Spelling Weekly Practice for 3rd Grade

Volume 1

Scholastic Panda
Education

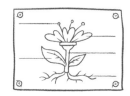

ISBN: 978-1-953149-45-9

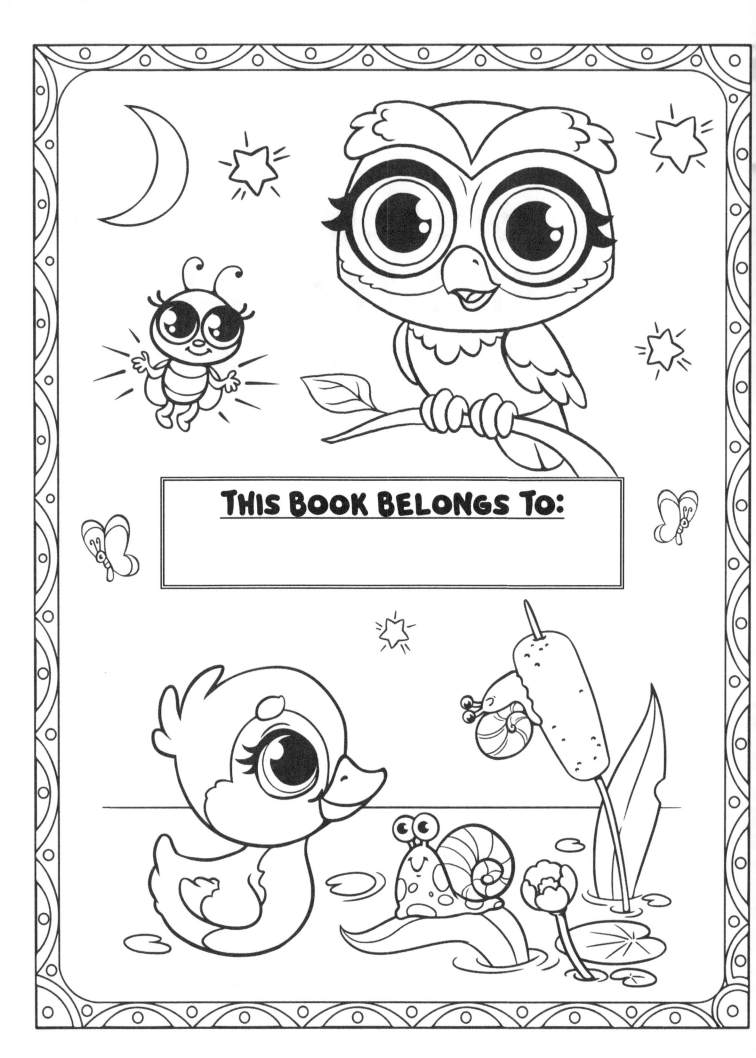

THIS BOOK BELONGS TO:

HELLO!

We are so excited to learn 3rd grade spelling words together!

- Inside you'll find 25 week of fun spelling units
- Each unit has 4 pages of exercises to practice

REMEMBER TO:

- Look at each spelling word
- Say the word out loud
- Write the word
- Color all of the fun doodles
- Have tons of fun!

DIGITAL ANSWER KEY

Found at the back of the book

Free Coloring Book for Kids!

This fun printable coloring book is a blast and keeps kids engaged for hours!

It's filled with cute doodles, animals, and so much more!

Get Your Copy Here:

https://bit.ly/3CMYsTO

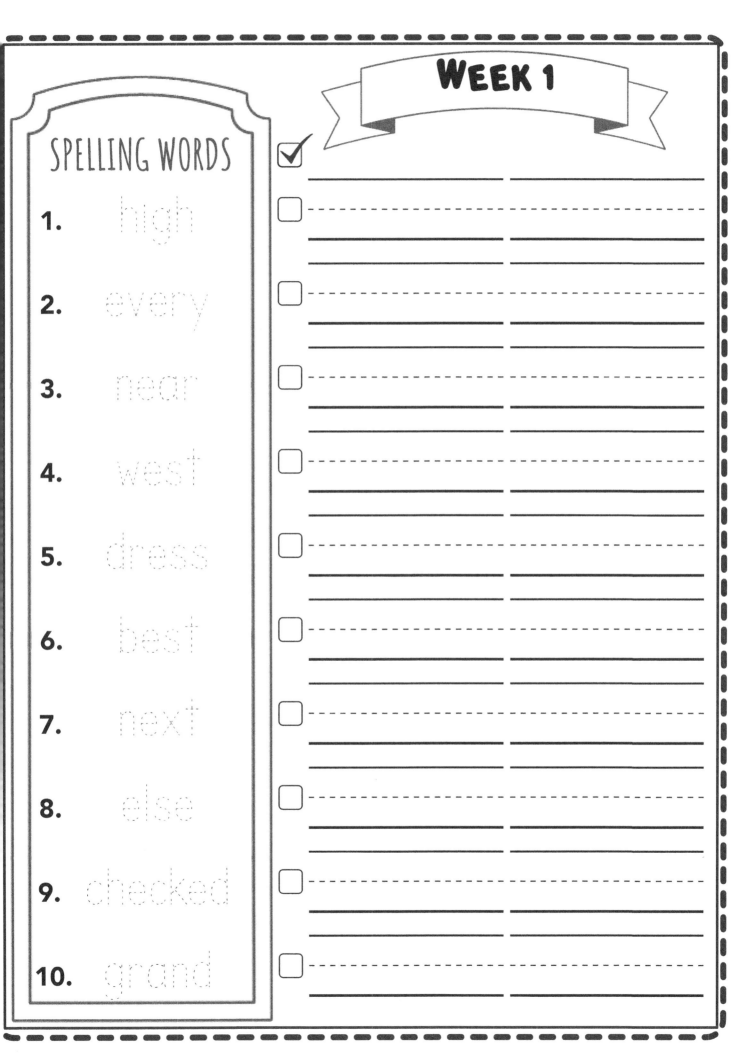

WEEK 1

SPELLING WORDS

1. high
2. every
3. near
4. west
5. dress
6. best
7. next
8. else
9. checked
10. grand

COLOR IN THE CIRCLES YOU NEED TO SPELL EACH WORD IN THE BOX. UNSCRAMBLE THE LEFTOVER CIRCLES TO SPELL A WORD FROM THIS WEEK.

| checked | grand | best | near | every | dress |

E
R C A D K H G N H
S T E D R Y E B C
E R A E R I E V N
H E D S G S

Write the hidden word here:

_____

Fill in the blanks using the words below. You will not use all of the words.

| checked | | best | | every | | else |
| high | grand | | west | near | | dress | next |

1. I _____ the oven to make sure I turned it off.

2. The movie theater is _____ my house.

3. What _____ do you enjoy doing?

4. I always try to do my _____ .

5. What direction is opposite of east? _____

Circle this week's correct spelling word in each row

1. everie   eveery   every   evury

2. highe   hie   hye   high

3. checked   cheked   chekced   chekked

4. ehlse   ellse   else   ellhse

5. grrand   grande   graand   grand

Unscramble the words and write the correct spelling on the line

NRAE _____   WSTE _____

ESRSD _____   BTSE _____

ENXT _____   ESEL _____

ECDCHKE _____   GNDRA _____

WEEK 1

Help the bees put the spelling words in alphabetical order

Don't forget to color the doodles!

WEEK 2

SPELLING WORDS

1. stand
2. punish
3. monarch
4. migrate
5. butterfly
6. nectar
7. between
8. own
9. base
10. country

Look at the letters in the shapes and then answer the questions below

a n   n a d s   e   r

c   c   t   u   r
    y   n   o   t

1. **What word can you make with the letters in the rectangle?**

_____

2. **What word can you make with the letters in the hexagon?**

_____

3. **What word can you make with the letters outside both shapes?**

_____

Unscramble the words and write the correct spelling on the line

RTNUCYO _____   ETRUTBFLY _____

SIHNPU _____   CANTRE _____

CHNAMRO _____   BNEEETW _____

TRAMGEI _____   ASEB _____

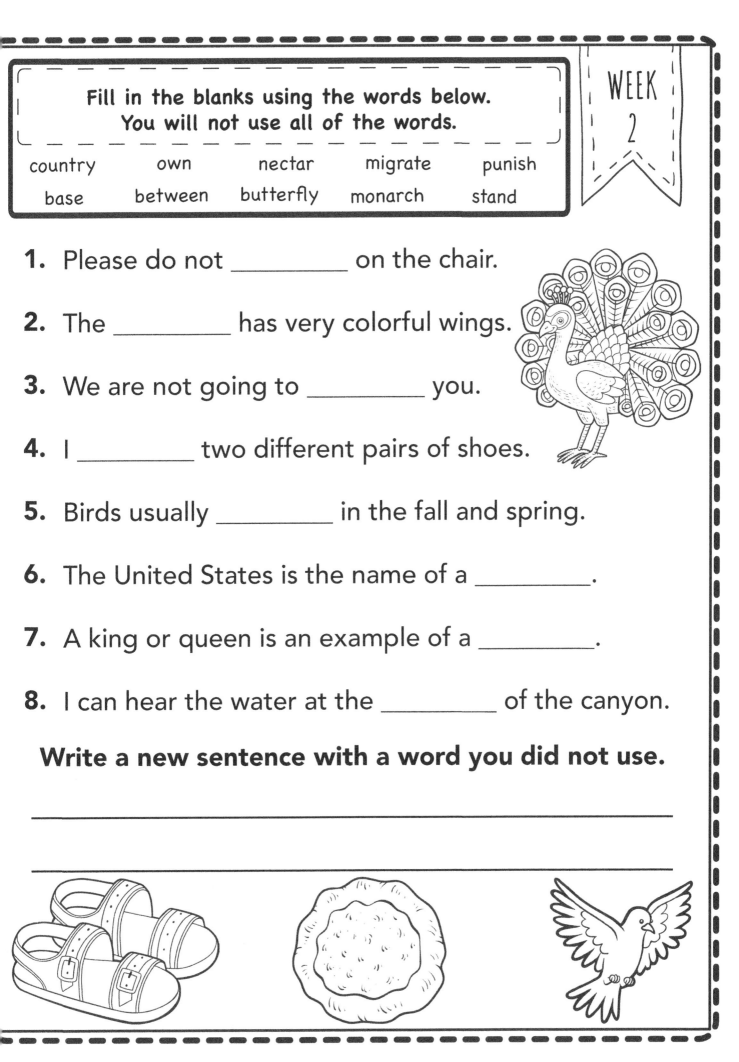

**Fill in the blanks using the words below.
You will not use all of the words.**

country   own   nectar   migrate   punish

base   between   butterfly   monarch   stand

1. Please do not _____ on the chair.

2. The _____ has very colorful wings.

3. We are not going to _____ you.

4. I _____ two different pairs of shoes.

5. Birds usually _____ in the fall and spring.

6. The United States is the name of a _____.

7. A king or queen is an example of a _____.

8. I can hear the water at the _____ of the canyon.

Write a new sentence with a word you did not use.

_____

_____

Use the letters that are shown in the crossword to help you fill in the rest of the puzzle with this week's spelling words. Cross off each word as you use it and write it again in the blank

3 across: S

4 across: U

5 across / down: R

6 down / 5: I

7 across: N   A

8 down

9 across: N

STAND _____

PUNISH _____

MONARCH _____

MIGRATE _____

BUTTERFLY _____

NECTAR _____

BETWEEN _____

OWN _____

BASE _____

COUNTRY _____

SPELLING WORDS

1. plant
2. slip
3. lunch
4. pond
5. front
6. thump
7. inches
8. yard
9. area
10. formula

Start at any letter and move around the circle, forward or backward, to find one of the spelling words.
Circle the first letter then write the full word below

P
L
A   1   T
N

H
E
C   2
N   S
I

P
M
U   3   T
H

L
A   U
F   4
O   M
R

N
C
H   5   U
L

⬥ ◇ ⬥ ◇ ⬥ ◇ ⬥ ◇ ⬥ ◇ ⬥ ◇ ⬥ ◇ ⬥

Circle this week's correct spelling word in each row

1. ponde   ponnd   pond   pand

2. yarde   yard   yurd   yarrd

3. formulah   forrmula   farmula   formula

4. area   areea   airea   aiirea

5. enches   inches   innches   inche

Circle each spelling word in the word search. Write each word twice in the blank spaces below as you find it.

G	E	A	C	F	T	I	L	H	F	I	N
M	T	F	W	P	A	O	I	H	R	I	P
U	X	F	J	P	D	E	G	B	O	J	M
C	U	M	L	H	C	V	R	G	N	F	O
Y	W	A	U	C	T	P	S	A	T	O	P
N	N	L	N	F	Z	E	E	Y	E	R	G
T	K	Z	C	P	M	U	H	T	Z	M	P
O	L	R	H	P	S	L	C	H	Y	U	H
F	V	Y	R	I	O	T	N	O	M	L	Y
D	R	T	T	L	T	N	I	Z	Y	A	A
E	W	F	E	S	J	J	D	A	U	Z	R
S	A	A	C	L	E	S	K	W	F	T	D

1 _____ _____   6 _____ _____

2 _____ _____   7 _____ _____

3 _____ _____   8 _____ _____

4 _____ _____   9 _____ _____

5 _____ _____   10 _____ _____

WEEK 3

Fill in the blanks using the words below.
You will not use all of the words.

formula   yard   thump   pond   slip

area   inches   front   lunch   plant

1. I had pizza for _____.

2. Twelve _____ equals one foot.

3. She went fishing at the _____.

4. He stood in _____ of the mirror.

5. The baby needs to drink a special _____.

6. Something fell because I heard a loud _____.

7. Do not run too fast because you could _____.

8. There are many ice cream shops in the _____.

Write a new sentence with a word you did not use.

_____

_____

SPELLING WORDS

1. width
2. calculate
3. save
4. school
5. father
6. keep
7. safe
8. grade
9. reached
10. raise

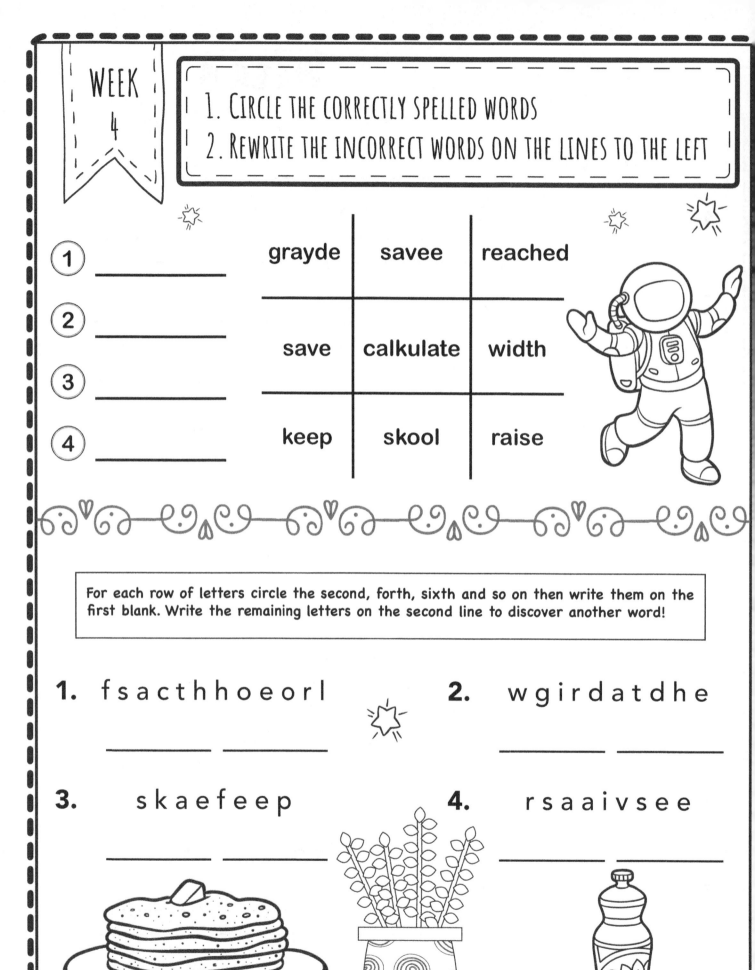

1. CIRCLE THE CORRECTLY SPELLED WORDS
2. REWRITE THE INCORRECT WORDS ON THE LINES TO THE LEFT

(1) _____

(2) _____

(3) _____

(4) _____

grayde	savee	reached
save	calkulate	width
keep	skool	raise

For each row of letters circle the second, forth, sixth and so on then write them on the first blank. Write the remaining letters on the second line to discover another word!

1. f s a c t h h o e o r l

_____

_____

2. w g i r d a t d h e

_____

_____

3. s k a e f e e p

_____

_____

4. r s a a i v s e e

_____

_____

COLOR IN THE CIRCLES YOU NEED TO SPELL EACH WORD IN THE BOX.
UNSCRAMBLE THE LEFTOVER CIRCLES TO SPELL A WORD FROM THIS WEEK.

| raise | reached | keep | calculate | safe |

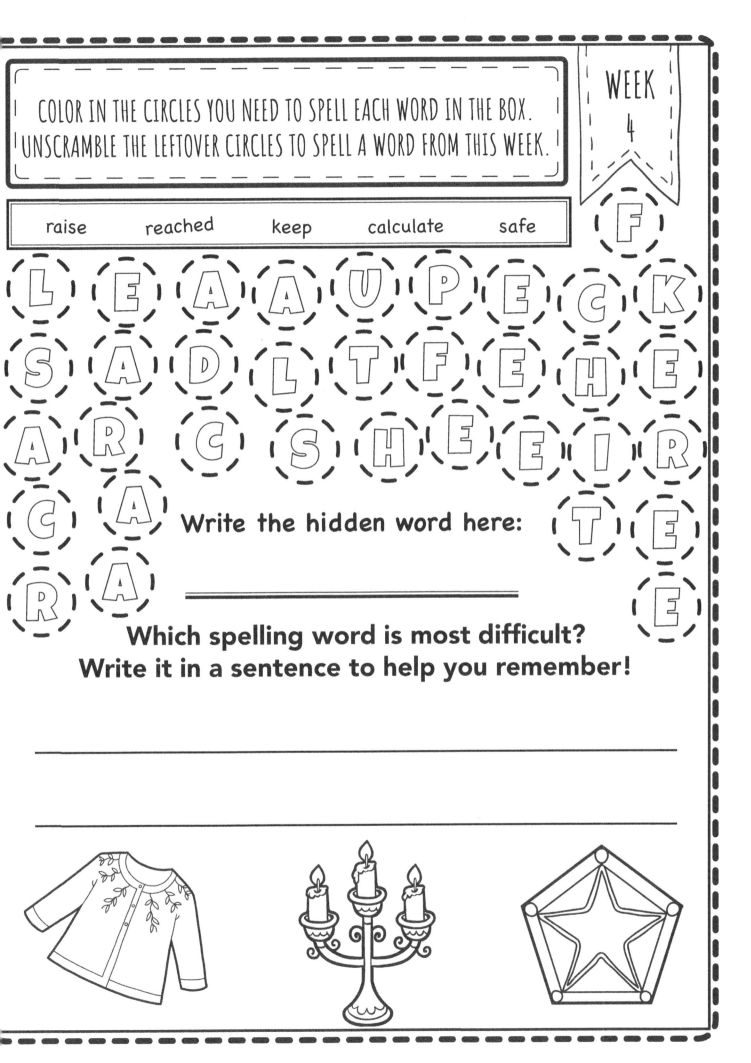

Write the hidden word here:

_____

Which spelling word is most difficult?
Write it in a sentence to help you remember!

_____

_____

WEEK 4

Color the word in each row that rhymes with the word on the left

SWEEP	nickel	keep	dust
WAVE	save	plant	turkey
POOL	weird	noodle	school
STAYED	bag	grade	hair
BLAZE	raise	swim	dolphin
GREAT	tire	keyboard	calculate

WEEK 5

SPELLING WORDS

1. theme
2. scream
3. easy
4. highway
5. navigate
6. ocean
7. travel
8. direction
9. trade
10. start

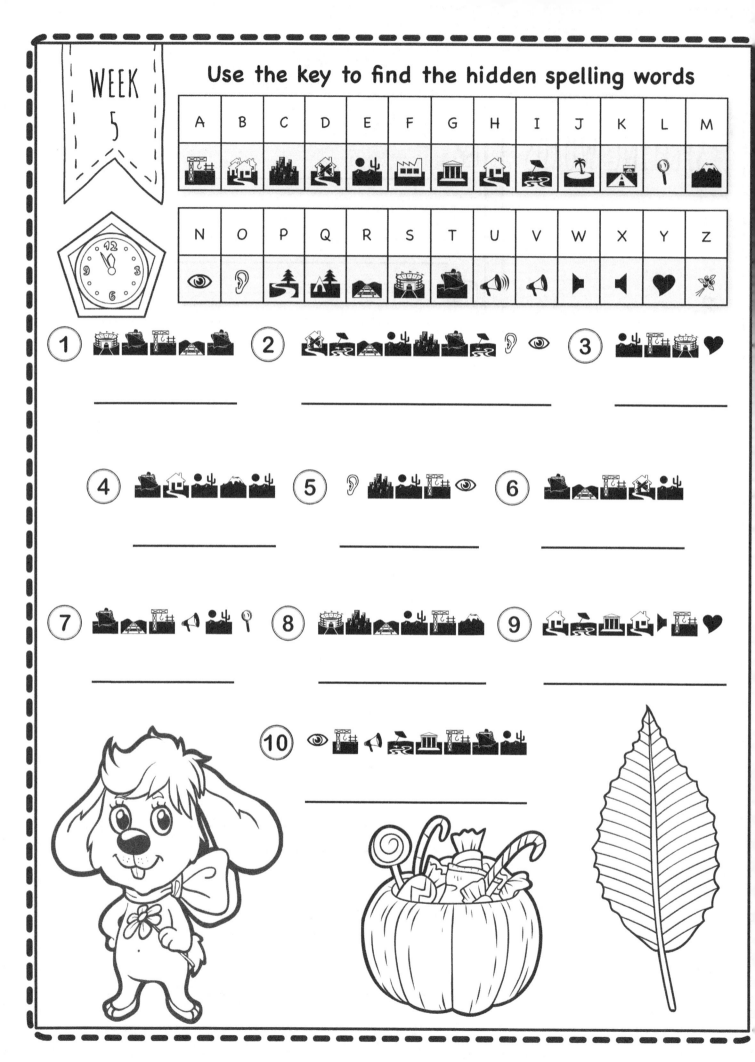

WEEK 5

Use the key to find the hidden spelling words

A	B	C	D	E	F	G	H	I	J	K	L	M

N	O	P	Q	R	S	T	U	V	W	X	Y	Z

1.

2.

3.

4.

5.

6.

7.

8.

9.

10.

Put all of the spelling words
in alphabetical order

WEEK
5

1. _____

2. _____

3. _____

4. _____

5. _____

6. _____

7. _____

8. _____

9. _____

10. _____

Start at any letter and move around the
circle to find one of the spelling words. Circle
the first letter then write the full word below

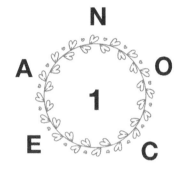
N
A   O
1
E   C

H
I   Y
G   A
2
H   W

_____   _____

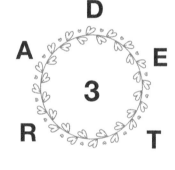
D
A   E
3
R   T

V
A   I
N   G
3
E   A
T

_____   _____

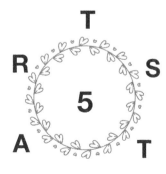
T
R   S
5
A   T

E
R   C
I   T
6
D   I
N   O

_____   _____

This astronaut loves tacos! Write a spelling word in each tacos and then have fun coloring them!

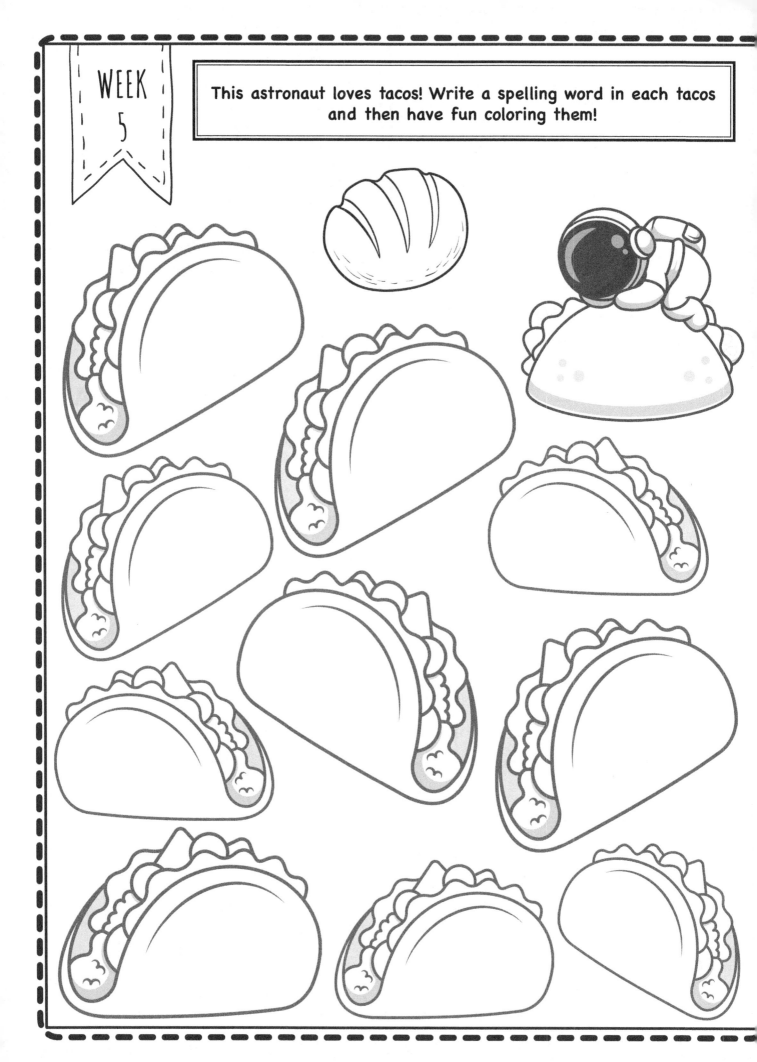

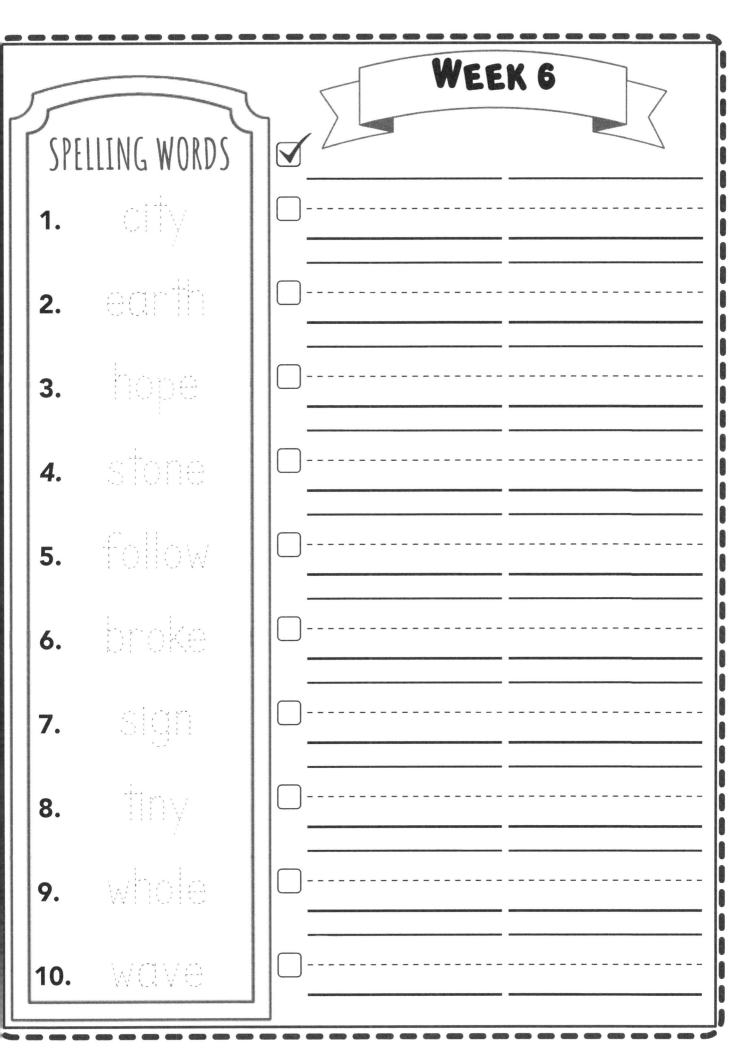

WEEK 6

SPELLING WORDS

1. city
2. earth
3. hope
4. stone
5. follow
6. broke
7. sign
8. tiny
9. whole
10. wave

Circle each spelling word in the word search. Write each word twice in the blank spaces below as you find it.

J	X	S	W	P	O	B	N	T	I	N	Y
S	W	O	K	A	E	N	O	T	S	N	V
K	A	F	O	K	S	X	S	Q	G	P	G
H	N	W	O	F	O	L	L	O	W	R	F
O	B	R	Z	T	A	W	Y	G	O	C	D
P	B	W	M	W	B	A	W	H	N	H	S
E	G	N	A	J	W	V	I	N	V	O	J
B	S	Q	T	C	T	E	D	H	A	G	E
L	C	S	H	K	A	A	F	S	L	J	B
N	I	S	I	G	N	R	M	O	X	A	L
V	T	Q	L	C	R	T	B	G	J	A	M
F	Y	W	E	L	O	H	W	C	S	B	K

1 _____ _____

2 _____ _____

3 _____ _____

4 _____ _____

5 _____ _____

6 _____ _____

7 _____ _____

8 _____ _____

9 _____ _____

10 _____ _____

Unscramble the words and write the correct spelling on the line

TYIC _____ LFOWLO _____

EHART _____ BREOK _____

HOEP _____ ISNG _____

OENST _____ NITY _____

Look at the letters in the shapes and then answer the questions below

a   l o f   e   r
     o l
   h   e w l   h   t
   h   o

1. **What word can you make with the letters in the triangle?**

_____

2. **What word can you make with the letters in the rectangle?**

_____

3. **What word can you make with the letters outside both shapes?**

_____

Fill in the blanks using the words below.
You will not use all of the words.

wave	sign	broke	stone	earth
whole	tiny	follow	hope	city

1. I will show you the way, please _____ me.

2. Chicago is also called the windy _____.

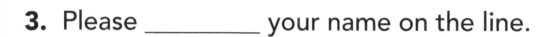

3. Please _____ your name on the line.

4. Some statues are made of _____.

5. That ladybug is so _____!

6. I really _____ you like my cooking.

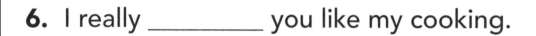

7. _____ is the third planet from the sun.

8. Are you going to eat the _____ pizza by yourself?

Write a new sentence with a word you did not use.

_____

_____

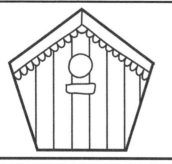

WEEK 7

SPELLING WORDS

1. current
2. electric
3. science
4. round
5. upon
6. thought
7. gun
8. strong
9. story
10. burst

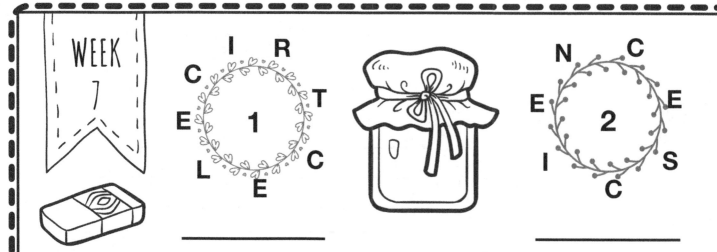

WEEK 7

CIRCLE 1

SENTENCE 2

_____

_____

sun	about	feed	gun
WRONG	near	strong	under
WORST	burst	happy	learn
SOUND	publish	round	grew
GLORY	race	skate	story
DRAWN	coffee	upon	addition

Use the letters that are shown in the crossword to help you fill in the rest of the puzzle with this week's spelling words. Cross off each word as you use it and write it again in the blank

BURST _____

STORY _____

STRONG _____   UPON _____

GUN _____   ROUND _____

THOUGHT _____   SCIENCE _____

ELECTRIC _____

CURRENT _____

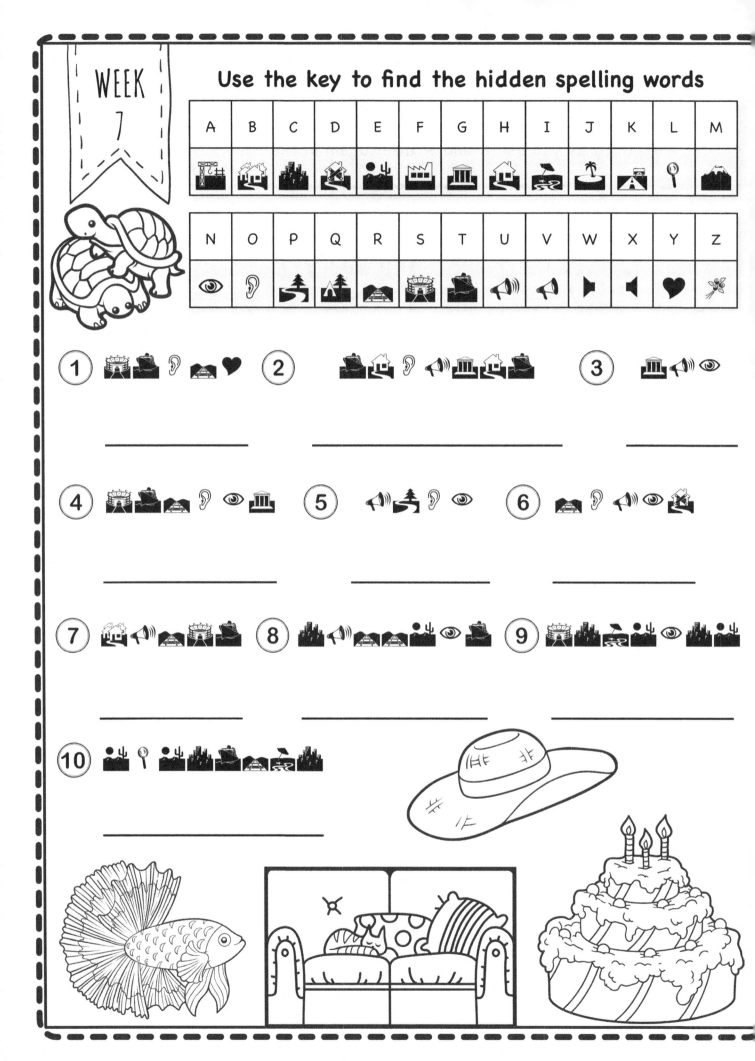

WEEK 7

Use the key to find the hidden spelling words

A	B	C	D	E	F	G	H	I	J	K	L	M

N	O	P	Q	R	S	T	U	V	W	X	Y	Z

1 _____

2 _____

3 _____

4 _____

5 _____

6 _____

7 _____

8 _____

9 _____

10 _____

SPELLING WORDS

1. strip
2. stream
3. street
4. distance
5. least
6. hundred
7. east
8. zero
9. nothing
10. amount

1. CIRCLE THE CORRECTLY SPELLED WORDS
2. REWRITE THE INCORRECT WORDS ON THE LINES TO THE LEFT

1 _____

2 _____

3 _____

4 _____

stream	amaunt	hundred
nothing	easte	strip
zeero	street	leest

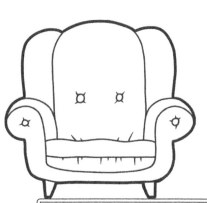

Unscramble the words and write the correct spelling on the line

UTMAON _____

NITGOHN _____

REZO _____

AETS _____

DUNERDH _____

LAETS _____

NCISEADT _____

TRTSEE _____

TRSAEM _____

IRSTP _____

**Fill in the blanks using the words below.
You will not use all of the words.**

nothing	zero	hundred	stream	distance
amount	east	strip	street	least

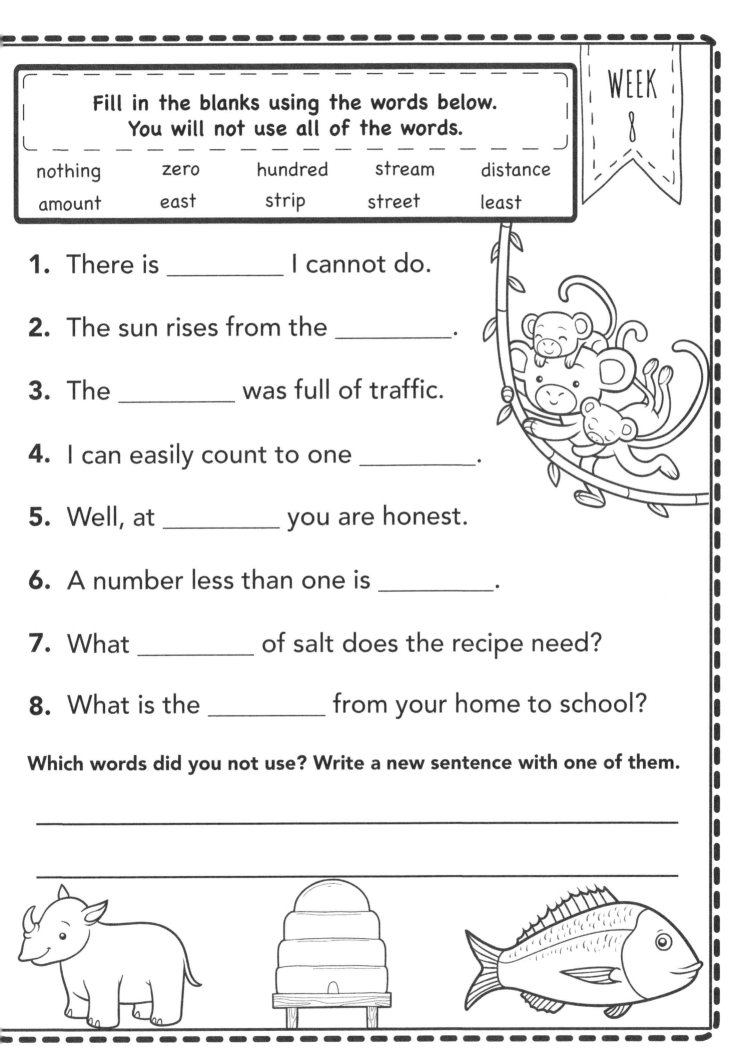

1. There is _____ I cannot do.

2. The sun rises from the _____.

3. The _____ was full of traffic.

4. I can easily count to one _____.

5. Well, at _____ you are honest.

6. A number less than one is _____.

7. What _____ of salt does the recipe need?

8. What is the _____ from your home to school?

Which words did you not use? Write a new sentence with one of them.

_____

_____

Correctly spell the words by filling in the blanks with the missing letters. Letters from the box below can be used more than once.

| H | T | A | S | N | I | L | M | O | G | Z | U | E |

S__RE__M

__TR__E__

D__S__ __ __CE

__EAS__

A__OU__T

N__T__IN__

__ERO

H__ __DR__D

Put each spelling word into alphabetical order and then write it again on the second line

1 _____ _____

2 _____ _____

3 _____ _____

4 _____ _____

5 _____ _____

6 _____ _____

7 _____ _____

8 _____ _____

9 _____ _____

10 _____ _____

WEEK 9

SPELLING WORDS

1. cried
2. dried
3. milk
4. let's
5. while
6. known
7. knife
8. knock
9. wrong
10. knot

Circle each spelling word in the word search.
Write each word twice in the blank spaces below as you find it.

H	F	U	I	M	T	W	U	F	J	L	S
M	I	A	S	S	E	F	I	N	K	R	A
K	J	K	P	Z	M	S	C	N	R	W	H
W	R	O	N	G	Z	X	T	V	T	C	M
L	H	P	Y	O	E	T	H	E	F	I	G
G	L	G	D	B	C	C	V	X	L	I	R
I	H	C	K	N	K	K	X	K	D	S	P
E	S	N	D	W	H	I	L	E	E	Q	I
U	O	Z	M	O	O	L	K	U	I	J	J
T	Q	Y	D	N	C	K	J	Y	R	M	W
T	X	J	Z	K	W	Z	X	G	D	I	E
G	C	R	I	E	D	U	T	F	D	K	D

1 _____   6 _____

2 _____   7 _____

3 _____   8 _____

4 _____   9 _____

5 _____   10 _____

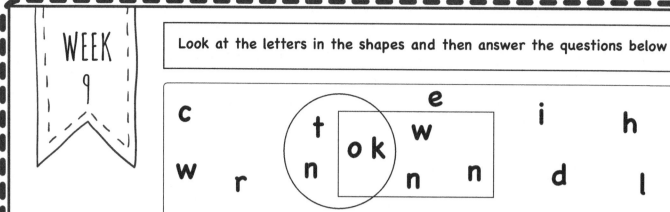

Look at the letters in the shapes and then answer the questions below

c
w
r
t
n
o k
e
w
n
n
i
h
d
l

1. **What word can you make with the letters in the circle?**

_____

2. **What word can you make with the letters in the rectangle?**

_____

3. **What two words can you make with the letters outside both shapes?**

_____   _____

Start at any letter and move around the circle to find one of the spelling words.
Circle the first letter then write the full word below

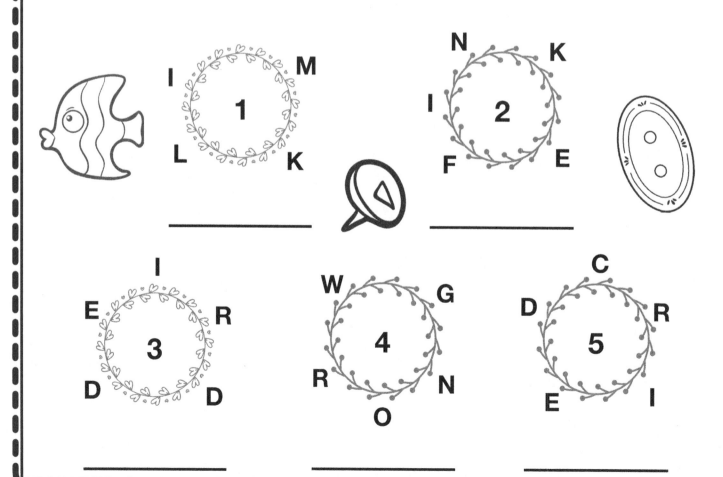

I   M
1
L   K

N   K
I   2   E
F

_____   _____

I
E   R
3
D   D

W   G
4
R   N
O

C
D   R
5
E   I

_____   _____   _____

SPELLING WORDS

1. wrinkle
2. wrap
3. wrist
4. knee
5. aloud
6. express
7. along
8. bought
9. close
10. something

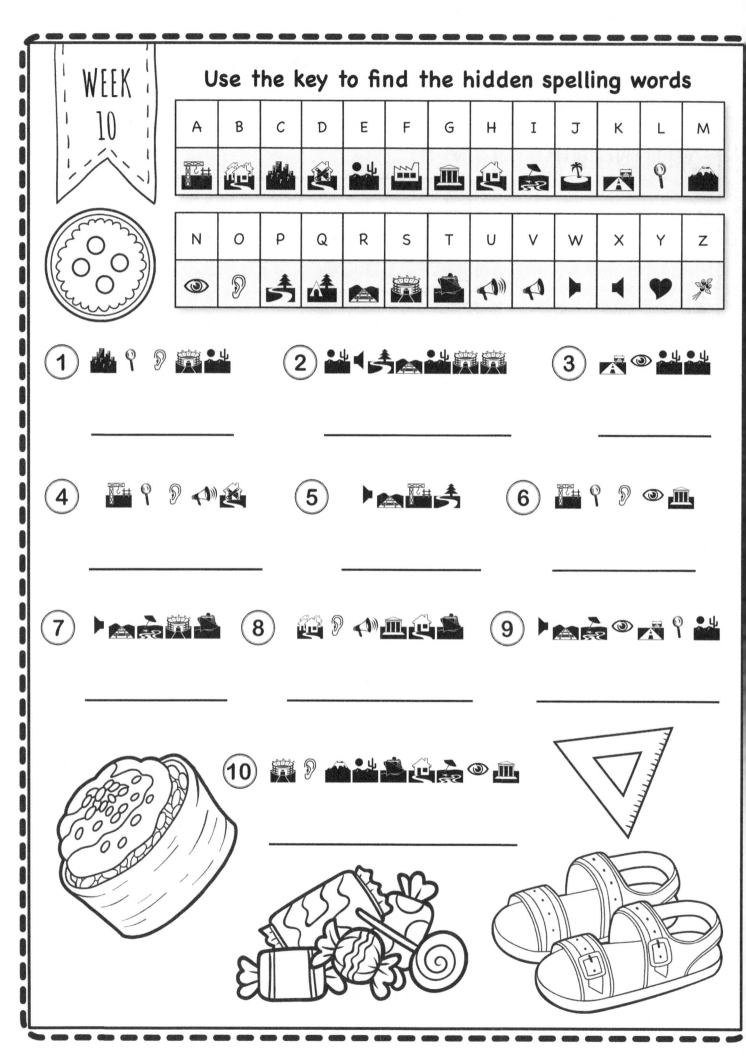

WEEK 10

Use the key to find the hidden spelling words

A	B	C	D	E	F	G	H	I	J	K	L	M

N	O	P	Q	R	S	T	U	V	W	X	Y	Z

1 _____

2 _____

3 _____

4 _____

5 _____

6 _____

7 _____

8 _____

9 _____

10 _____

Fill in the blanks using the words below.
You will not use all of the words.

something	bought	aloud	knee	wrap
close	along	express	wrist	wrinkle

1. Please read the story _____.

2. The _____ helps the leg bend.

3. We rode our bikes _____ the beach.

4. I need to iron my shirt, it has a _____.

5. _____ tells me you are in a good mood.

6. She _____ her friend a present for her birthday.

7. We were very _____ to the stage at the concert.

8. It is important to _____ your feelings some times.

What is your favorite word this week?
Write a new sentence with it!

_____

_____

Correctly spell the words by filling in the blanks with the missing letters. Letters from the box below can be used more than once.

H R S N W T N O L M E

B__UG__T   S__ __ __THI__G

EXP__E__ __   AL__UD

AL__ __G   __RI__K__E

W_IS__   CL__S__

Write each spelling word in alphabetical order on the xylophone and then color each bar with a different color!

SPELLING WORDS

1. seem
2. laughed
3. lady
4. enough
5. graph
6. paragraph
7. photograph
8. history
9. village
10. future

Color the word in each row that rhymes with the word on the left

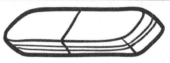

BEAM	weather	seem	dust
TOUGH	time	bright	enough
MYSTERY	history	brown	spell
SHADY	noun	lady	orange
CRAFT	cake	bricks	laughed
STAFF	graph	blanket	socks

Circle each spelling word in the word search. Write each word twice in the blank spaces below as you find it.

WEEK 11

J	P	H	O	T	O	G	R	A	P	H	K
H	G	U	O	N	E	B	X	O	F	B	W
Q	B	I	P	Z	F	U	T	U	R	E	T
C	P	R	A	R	D	U	U	S	Y	G	A
M	R	B	H	P	A	R	G	A	R	A	P
A	K	E	G	O	T	S	J	S	J	L	T
Y	X	J	H	D	E	H	G	U	A	L	S
D	N	S	E	D	H	L	X	S	S	I	E
A	N	U	B	P	Y	B	V	C	W	V	E
L	Z	I	A	R	S	K	M	I	U	J	M
G	Y	R	K	S	V	C	E	Z	W	P	Q
T	G	Q	H	I	S	T	O	R	Y	X	Z

1 _____ _____

2 _____ _____

3 _____ _____

4 _____ _____

5 _____ _____

6 _____ _____

7 _____ _____

8 _____ _____

9 _____ _____

10 _____ _____

1. CIRCLE THE CORRECTLY SPELLED WORDS
2. REWRITE THE INCORRECT WORDS ON THE LINES TO THE LEFT

1 _____

2 _____

3 _____

4 _____

seem	enough	footure
history	fotograph	graph
village	ladie	laffed

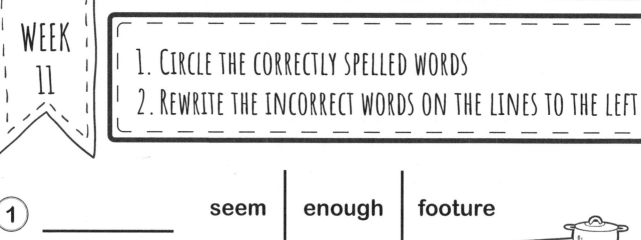

Unscramble the words and write the correct spelling on the line

TERFUU _____   RAHRPAGPA _____

AELILVG _____   ARGHP _____

IOTSRHY _____   YADL _____

ROHTOGHPPA _____   DHELUAG _____

GONEUH _____   EESM _____

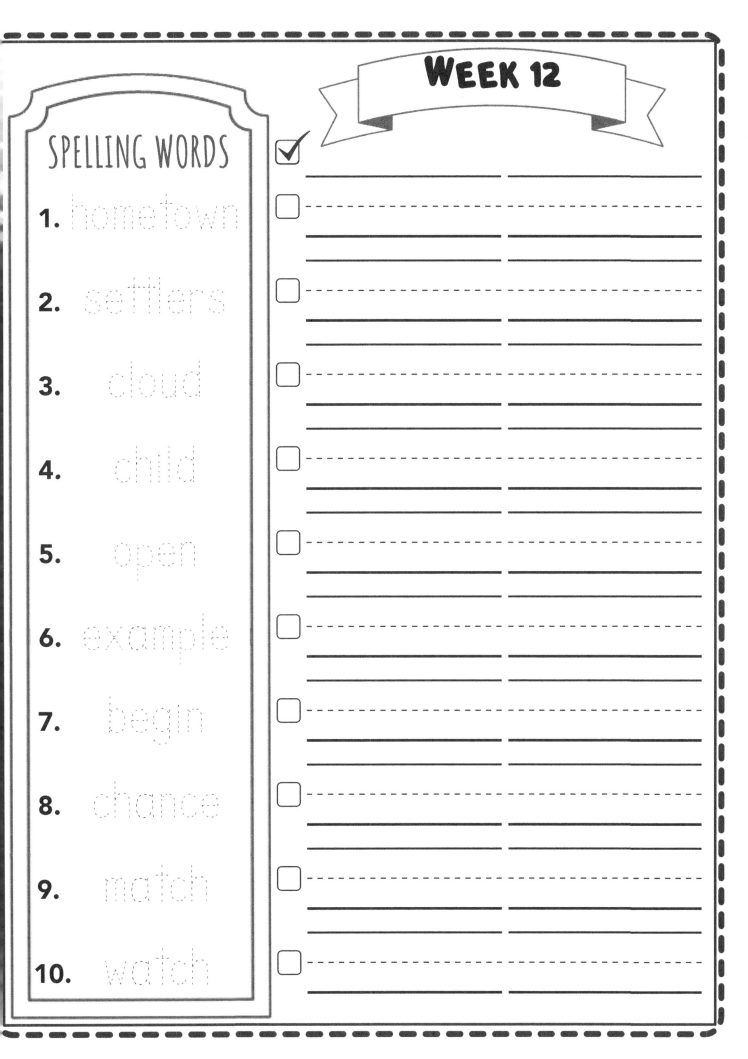

WEEK 12

SPELLING WORDS

1. hometown
2. settlers
3. cloud
4. child
5. open
6. example
7. begin
8. chance
9. match
10. watch

Use the letters that are shown in the crossword to help you fill in the rest of the puzzle with this week's spelling words. Cross off each word as you use it and write it again in the blank

HOMETOWN _____   SETTLERS _____

CLOUD _____   CHILD _____

OPEN _____   EXAMPLE _____

BEGIN _____   CHANCE _____

MATCH _____   WATCH _____

COLOR IN THE CIRCLES YOU NEED TO SPELL EACH WORD IN THE BOX.
UNSCRAMBLE THE LEFTOVER CIRCLES TO SPELL A WORD FROM THIS WEEK.

cloud   example   begin   chance   watch

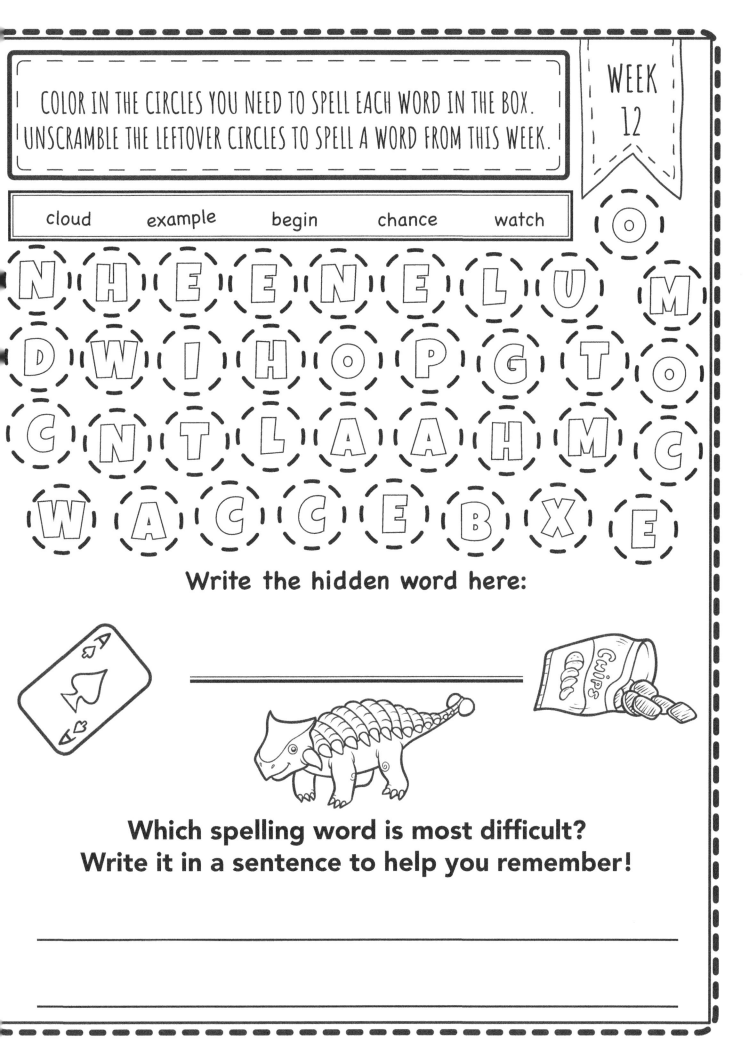

N H E E N E L U M
D W I H O P G T O
C N T L A A H M C
W A C C E B X E
O

Write the hidden word here:

_____

Which spelling word is most difficult?
Write it in a sentence to help you remember!

_____

_____

Fill in the blanks using the words below.
You will not use all of the words.

| cloud | open | begin | chance | watch |
| settlers | child | example | match | hometown |

1. My best friend's _____ is San Francisco, California.

2. I like your shoes, they _____ well with your shirt.

3. Is there a _____ you will be there tomorrow?

4. Please give me an _____ of what you mean.

5. The _____ was blocking the sun.

6. My _____ is broken, what time is it?.

7. The box is fragile so _____ it very carefully.

8. I am still a _____ but someday I will be an adult.

What is your favorite word this week?
Write a new sentence with it!

_____

_____

WEEK 13

SPELLING WORDS

1. batch
2. steel
3. speech
4. source
5. material
6. ditch
7. women
8. iron
9. can't
10. shall

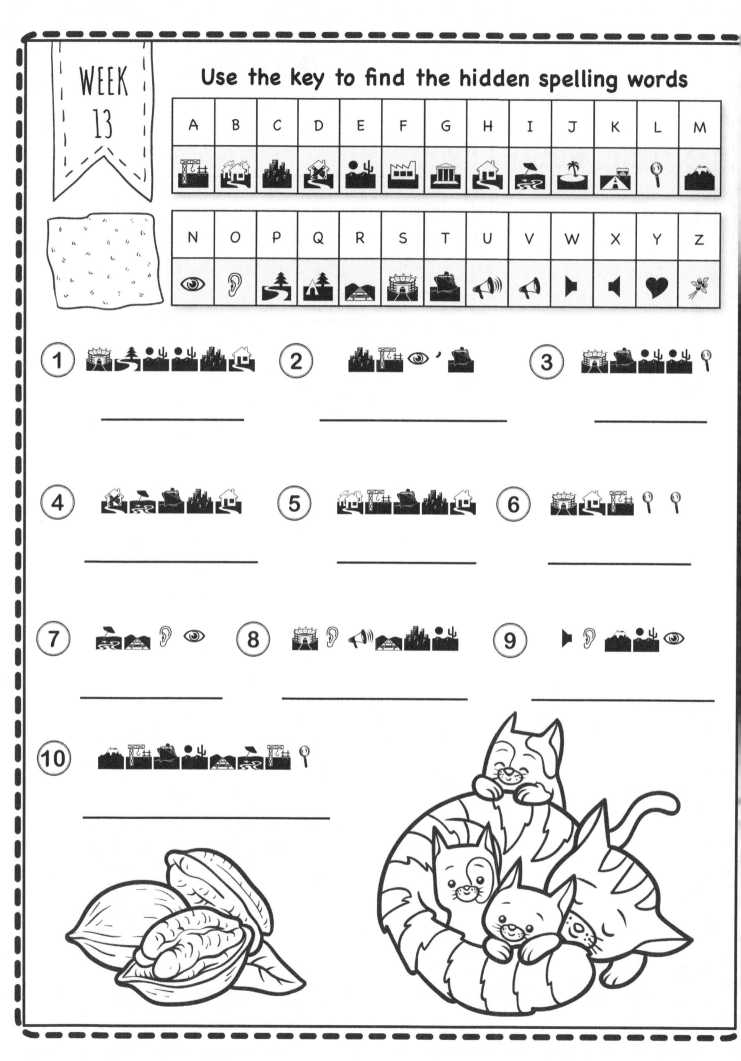

WEEK 13

Use the key to find the hidden spelling words

A	B	C	D	E	F	G	H	I	J	K	L	M

N	O	P	Q	R	S	T	U	V	W	X	Y	Z

1. _____
2. _____
3. _____
4. _____
5. _____
6. _____
7. _____
8. _____
9. _____
10. _____

Unscramble each word to complete the sentences.

1. I have to give a _____ (peshce) in front of my whole class.

2. My bed sheets are made of a high quality _____ (aeatirml).

3. My grandma made a fresh _____ (atbhc) of cookies.

4. _____ (sllah) we go see a movie in theater tonight?

5. I _____ (n'cta) ride the roller coaster yet, I am too short.

6. Steel is often used to make bridges, not _____ (roni).

7. Equality rights for _____ (omwne) is very important.

8. A car drove too fast and went into a _____ (tcdhi).

What is your favorite word this week? Write a new sentence with it!

_____

_____

WEEK 13

Put all of the spelling words into alphabetical order

Start at any letter and move around the circle to find one of the spelling words. Circle the first letter then write the full word below

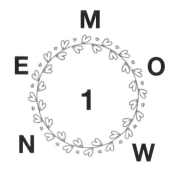

M
E   O
1
N   W

E
C   E
2
H   P
S

A
T   B
3
C   H

R
U   C
4
O   E
S

I
D   T
5
H   C

A
T   M
E   **6**
R   L
I   A

1. _____

2. _____

3. _____

4. _____

5. _____

6. _____

7. _____

8. _____

9. _____

10. _____

WEEK 14

SPELLING WORDS

1. those
2. both
3. paper
4. pushed
5. sharp
6. shock
7. crash
8. showed
9. shoes
10. shoulder

WEEK 14

Circle each spelling word in the word search.
Write each word twice in the blank spaces below as you find it.

M	F	R	X	F	U	W	Y	F	U	W	P
J	X	I	P	Y	Z	J	O	N	R	A	L
L	Y	W	R	D	E	H	S	U	P	S	T
Y	E	F	A	S	N	H	Z	E	H	B	T
X	E	H	H	L	O	J	R	O	C	C	V
T	J	C	S	W	M	G	U	E	N	H	I
J	J	R	E	H	O	L	K	O	Y	O	G
H	A	D	T	D	D	V	M	C	N	G	P
S	Q	O	S	E	A	A	E	S	O	H	T
A	B	H	R	H	L	B	Q	R	W	H	T
R	X	M	V	S	H	O	E	S	Z	V	S
C	C	Z	B	A	A	J	T	D	X	I	S

1 _____ _____

2 _____ _____

3 _____ _____

4 _____ _____

5 _____ _____

6 _____ _____

7 _____ _____

8 _____ _____

9 _____ _____

10 _____ _____

COLOR IN THE CIRCLES YOU NEED TO SPELL EACH WORD IN THE BOX. UNSCRAMBLE THE LEFTOVER CIRCLES TO SPELL A WORD FROM THIS WEEK.

WEEK 14

| shock | those | paper | shoulder | sharp |

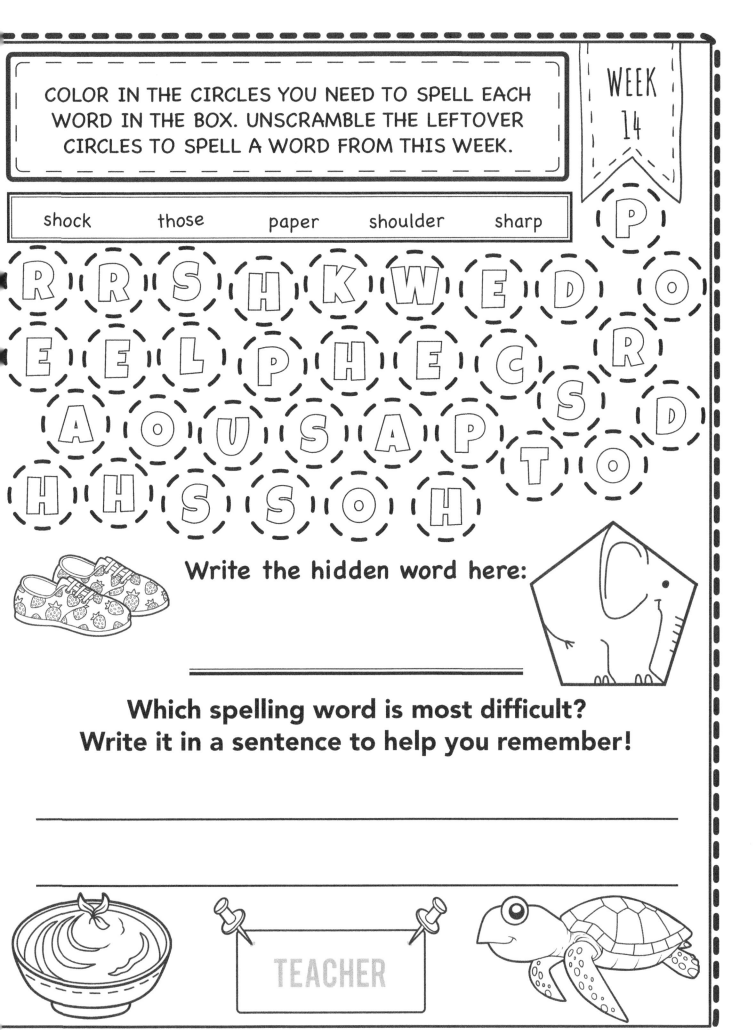

Write the hidden word here:

_____

Which spelling word is most difficult?
Write it in a sentence to help you remember!

_____

_____

TEACHER

Correctly spell the words by filling in the blanks with the missing letters. Letters from the box below can be used more than once.

H   S   C   B   O   L   E

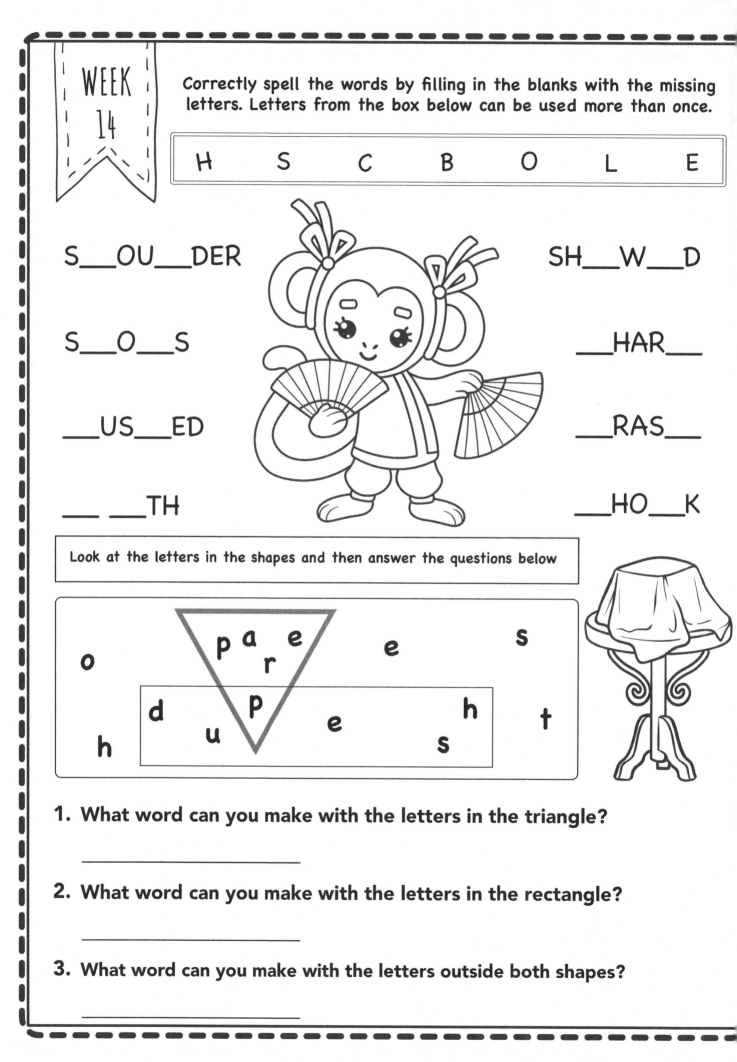

S__OU__DER

S__O__S

__US__ED

__ __TH

SH__W__D

__HAR__

__RAS__

__HO__K

Look at the letters in the shapes and then answer the questions below

o   p a e   e   s
        r
    d   u P   e   h   t
h   s

1. What word can you make with the letters in the triangle?

_____

2. What word can you make with the letters in the rectangle?

_____

3. What word can you make with the letters outside both shapes?

_____

SPELLING WORDS

1. product
2. quotient
3. multiplication
4. division
5. together
6. tied
7. group
8. often
9. table
10. space

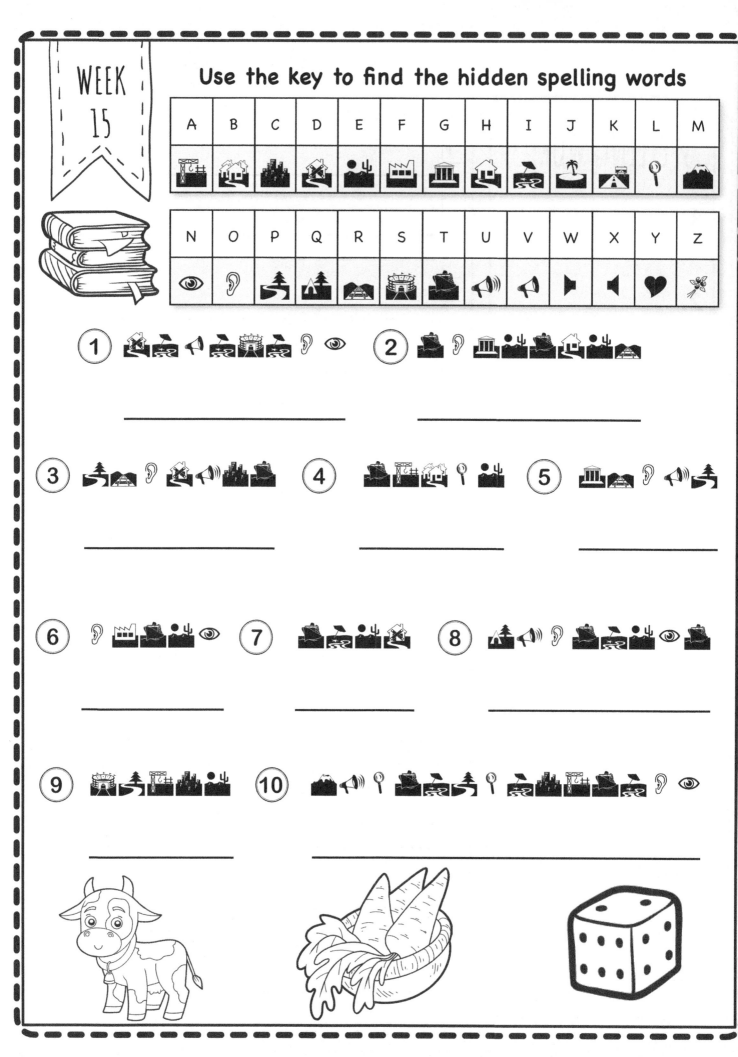

WEEK 15

Use the key to find the hidden spelling words

A	B	C	D	E	F	G	H	I	J	K	L	M

N	O	P	Q	R	S	T	U	V	W	X	Y	Z

1 _____

2 _____

3 _____

4 _____

5 _____

6 _____

7 _____

8 _____

9 _____

10 _____

Use the letters that are shown in the crossword to help you fill in the rest of the puzzle with this week's spelling words. Write each word on the blank as you use it

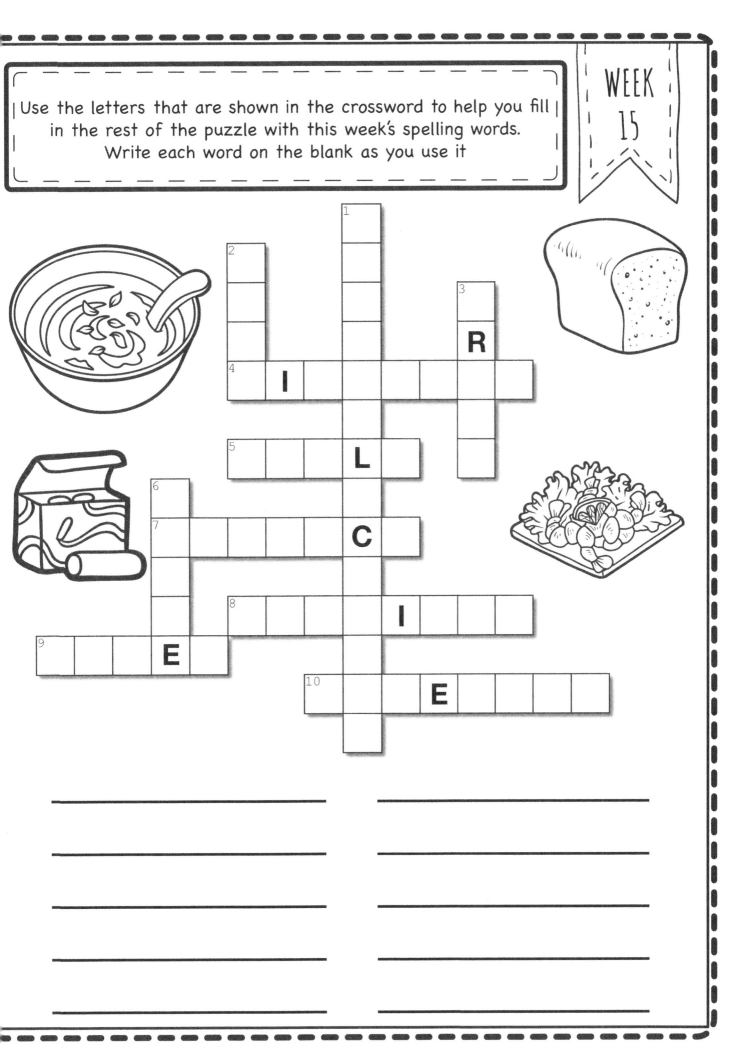

WEEK 15

Color the word in each row that rhymes with the word on the left

RACE	ego	space	outside
SOUP	dark	piano	group
WEATHER	slice	either	together
TELEVISION	square	division	sauce
BRIDE	tied	grid	jog
POTENT	fins	quotient	crown

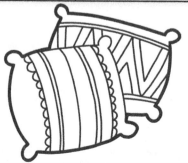

SPELLING WORDS

1. fence
2. price
3. office
4. police
5. pencil
6. civil
7. tribal
8. buffalo
9. dance
10. plains

WEEK 16

Circle each spelling word in the word search.
Write each word twice in the blank spaces below as you find it.

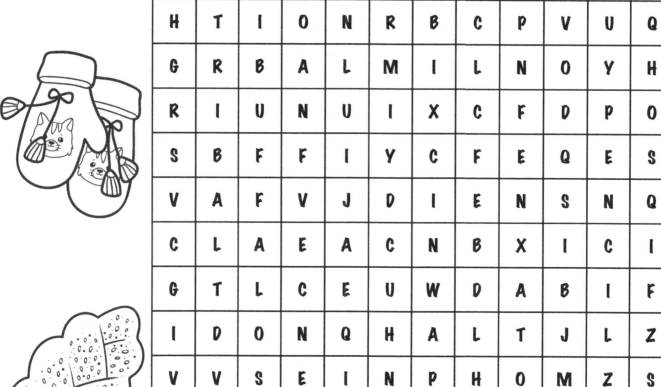

D	L	P	P	P	H	M	R	Q	Q	X	J
H	T	I	O	N	R	B	C	P	V	U	Q
G	R	B	A	L	M	I	L	N	O	Y	H
R	I	U	N	U	I	X	C	F	D	P	O
S	B	F	F	I	Y	C	F	E	Q	E	S
V	A	F	V	J	D	I	E	N	S	N	Q
C	L	A	E	A	C	N	B	X	I	C	I
G	T	L	C	E	U	W	D	A	B	I	F
I	D	O	N	Q	H	A	L	T	J	L	Z
V	V	S	E	I	N	P	H	O	M	Z	S
T	F	O	F	C	S	L	X	V	M	L	F
T	P	M	E	L	I	V	I	C	B	K	W

1 _____ _____   6 _____ _____

2 _____ _____   7 _____ _____

3 _____ _____   8 _____ _____

4 _____ _____   9 _____ _____

5 _____ _____   10 _____ _____

1. Circle the correctly spelled words
2. Rewrite the incorrect words on the lines to the left

WEEK 16

① _____

② _____

③ _____

④ _____

poleese	tribal	pencil
office	civul	price
buffelo	fence	playns

TURKEY TIME! Write each word alphabetically in the numbered feathers.
Make sure to color the turkey!

WEEK 16

Start at any letter and move around the circle to find one of the spelling words.
Circle the first letter then write the full word below

E
N   F
1
C   E

_____

L
O   A
B
2
    F
U
F

_____

C
N   I
3
E   L
P

_____

For each row of letters circle the second, forth, sixth and so on then write them on the first blank. Write the remaining letters on the second line to discover another word!

1. t c r i i v b i a l l

_____ _____

2. p p o l l a i i c n e s

_____ _____

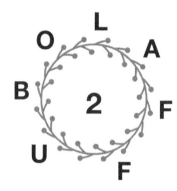

3. p d r a i n c c e e

_____ _____

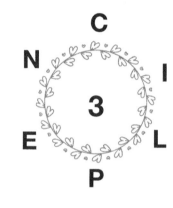

4. p f e e n n c c i e l

_____ _____

WEEK 17

SPELLING WORDS

1. important
2. cannot
3. children
4. wife
5. gentle
6. giraffe
7. hoe
8. stage
9. engine
10. badge

Use the letters that are shown in the crossword to help you fill in the rest of the puzzle with this week's spelling words. Write each word on the blank as you use it

COLOR IN THE CIRCLES YOU NEED TO SPELL EACH
WORD IN THE BOX. UNSCRAMBLE THE LEFTOVER
CIRCLES TO SPELL A WORD FROM THIS WEEK.

WEEK
17

wife   engine   children   cannot   important   badge

Write the hidden word here:

_____

Which spelling word is most difficult?
Write it in a sentence to help you remember!

_____

_____

Unscramble each word to complete the sentences.

1. A _____ (rgafief) has a very long neck.

2. My teacher's _____ (ewfi) is a scientist.

3. A _____ (ohe) it a tool used for gardening.

4. The band is about to take the _____ (etgas).

5. Most _____ (deihnclr) love eating ice cream.

6. A race car has a very powerful _____ (neineg).

7. When you hold a baby you must be very _____ (telnge).

8. It is very _____ (onttpaimr) to brush your teeth everyday.

**What is your favorite word this week?
Write a new sentence with it!**

_____

_____

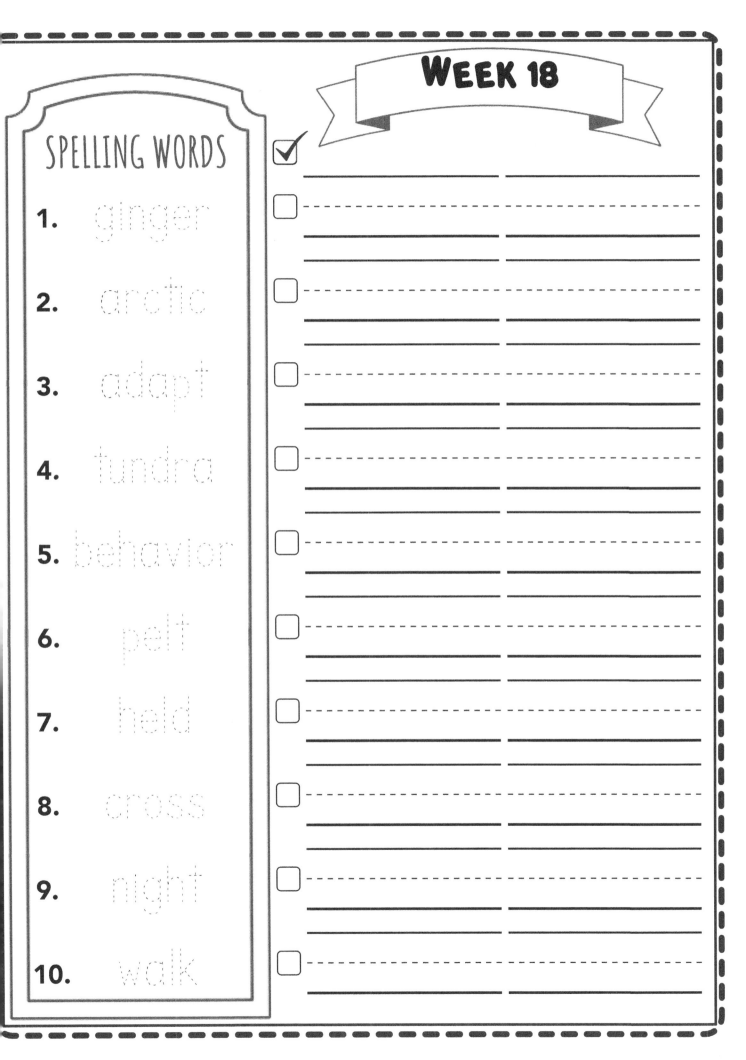

WEEK 18

SPELLING WORDS

1. ginger
2. arctic
3. adapt
4. tundra
5. behavior
6. pelt
7. held
8. cross
9. night
10. walk

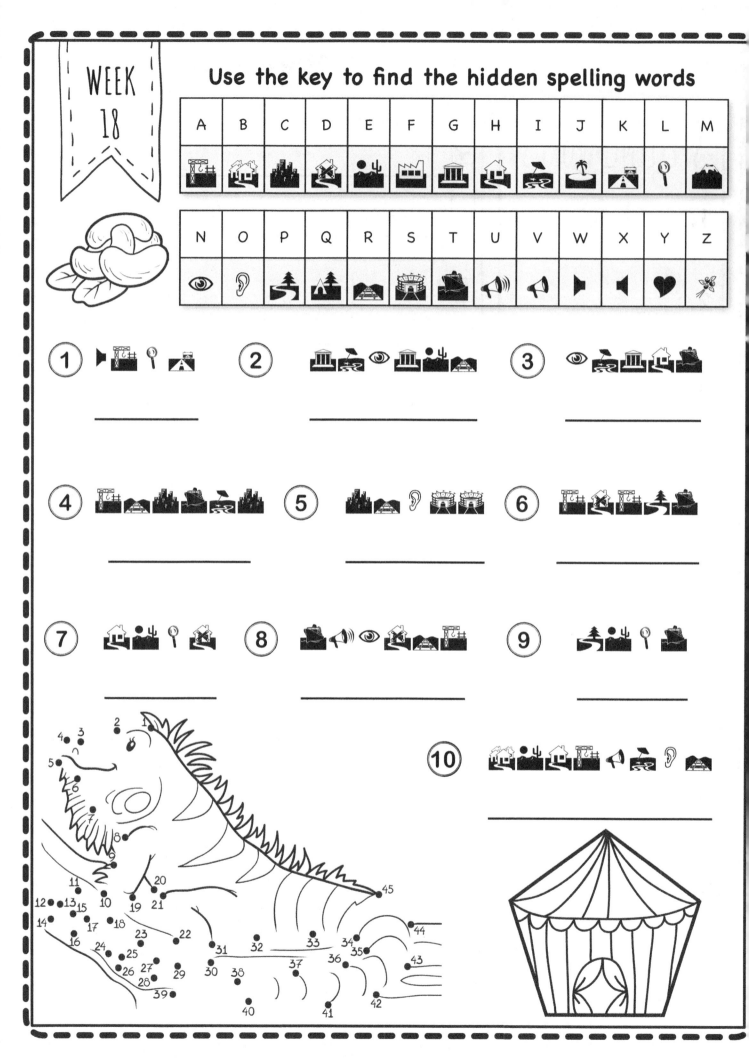

WEEK 18

Use the key to find the hidden spelling words

A	B	C	D	E	F	G	H	I	J	K	L	M

N	O	P	Q	R	S	T	U	V	W	X	Y	Z

1

2

3

4

5

6

7

8

9

10

Correctly spell the words by filling in the blanks with the missing letters. Letters from the box below can be used more than once.

O U S G D H P T I A K E B

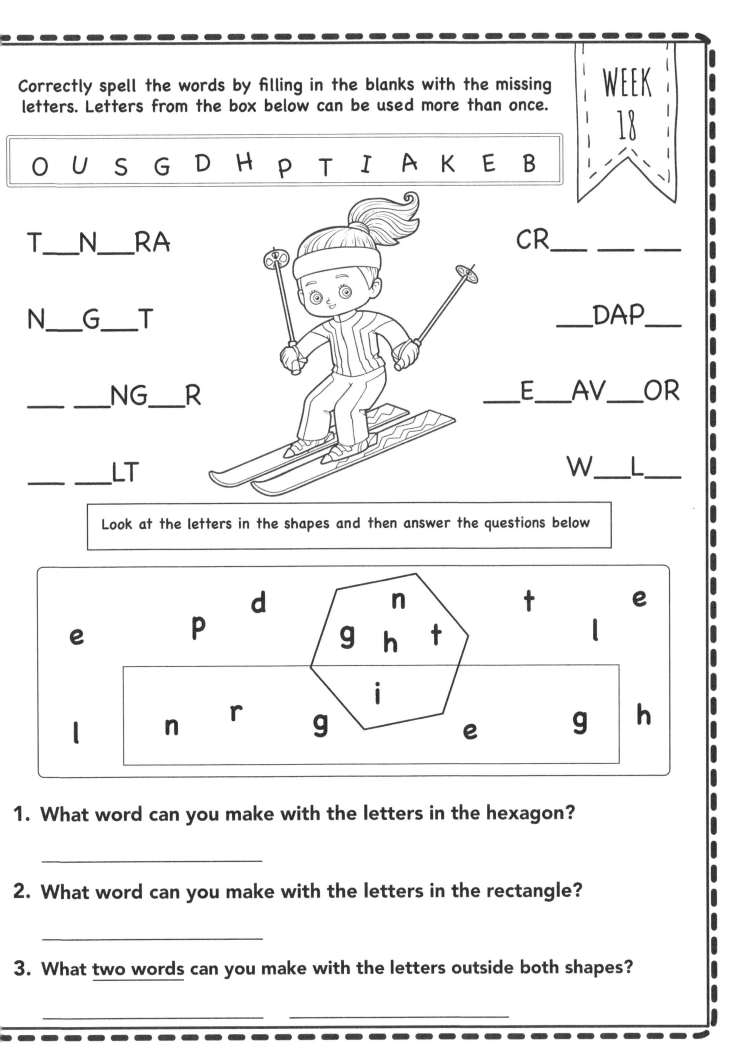

T__N__RA

N__G__T

__ __NG__R

__ __LT

CR__ __ __

__DAP__

__E__AV__OR

W__L__

Look at the letters in the shapes and then answer the questions below

1. **What word can you make with the letters in the hexagon?**

   _____

2. **What word can you make with the letters in the rectangle?**

   _____

3. **What two words can you make with the letters outside both shapes?**

   _____   _____

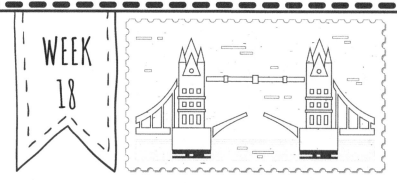

WEEK 18

Put all of the spelling words into alphabetical order

Start at any letter and move around the circle to find one of the spelling words. Circle the first letter then write the full word below

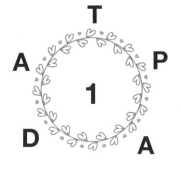

T
A   P
  1
D   A

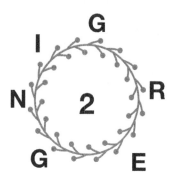

          G
I
N   R
  2
G   E

_____

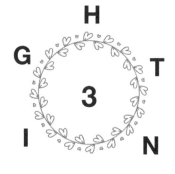

H
G   T
  3
I   N

      A
H   V
E   I
  4
B   O
      R

_____

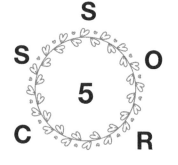

      S
S   O
  5
C   R

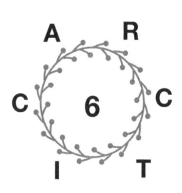

A   R
C   C
  6
I   T

_____

1. _____

2. _____

3. _____

4. _____

5. _____

6. _____

7. _____

8. _____

9. _____

10. _____

SPELLING WORDS

1. picked
2. choice
3. voice
4. royal
5. annoy
6. noise
7. tomato
8. potato
9. citrus
10. nutrients

Circle each spelling word in the word search.
Write each word twice in the blank spaces below as you find it.

R	W	Z	S	T	E	N	O	I	S	E	F
J	R	Z	T	O	Y	V	J	I	R	C	L
U	A	U	Z	M	C	F	B	C	N	I	A
Y	J	W	T	A	O	T	I	K	U	O	Y
F	P	P	O	T	A	T	O	C	T	H	O
D	U	I	Y	O	R	B	R	E	R	C	R
Z	V	Y	C	U	Z	G	B	P	I	H	C
V	R	O	S	K	X	D	Y	S	E	W	D
O	C	N	M	N	E	R	A	J	N	F	O
I	P	N	V	O	N	D	N	V	T	K	O
C	F	A	X	X	V	K	D	F	S	V	H
E	T	Y	Q	L	D	N	D	E	W	U	U

1 _____ _____

2 _____ _____

3 _____ _____

4 _____ _____

5 _____ _____

6 _____ _____

7 _____ _____

8 _____ _____

9 _____ _____

10 _____ _____

This sloth loves to paint and being creative.
Write a spelling word in each splash then color them!

WEEK 19

For each row of letters circle the second, forth, sixth and so on then write them on the first blank. Write the remaining letters on the second line to discover another word!

1. p c i h c o k i e c d e

_____

_____

2. r a o n y n a o l y

_____

_____

3. p c o i t t a r t u o s

_____

_____

4. n v o o i i s c e e

_____

_____

Circle this week's correct spelling word in each row

1. nootrents   nutrients   nutreents   nutriants

2. tomayto   toemato   tomato   tohmato

3. noise   noice   nohse   noyse

4. picced   pikced   picted   picked

5. voyse   voice   vosye   voise

WEEK 20

SPELLING WORDS

1. vitamins
2. vegetable
3. began
4. shouted
5. took
6. river
7. crown
8. however
9. around
10. growl

Unscramble each word to complete the sentences.

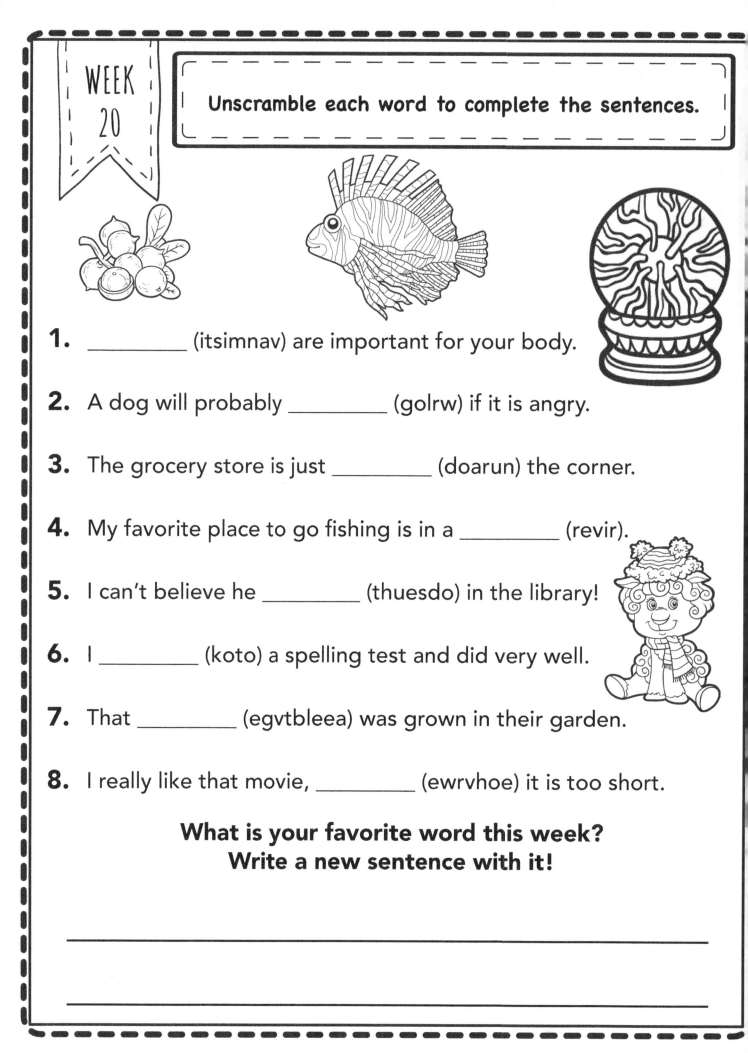

1. _____ (itsimnav) are important for your body.

2. A dog will probably _____ (golrw) if it is angry.

3. The grocery store is just _____ (doarun) the corner.

4. My favorite place to go fishing is in a _____ (revir).

5. I can't believe he _____ (thuesdo) in the library!

6. I _____ (koto) a spelling test and did very well.

7. That _____ (egvtbleea) was grown in their garden.

8. I really like that movie, _____ (ewrvhoe) it is too short.

What is your favorite word this week?
Write a new sentence with it!

_____

_____

COLOR IN THE CIRCLES YOU NEED TO SPELL EACH
WORD IN THE BOX. UNSCRAMBLE THE LEFTOVER
CIRCLES TO SPELL A WORD FROM THIS WEEK.

WEEK
20

shouted	vitamins	began	however	crown

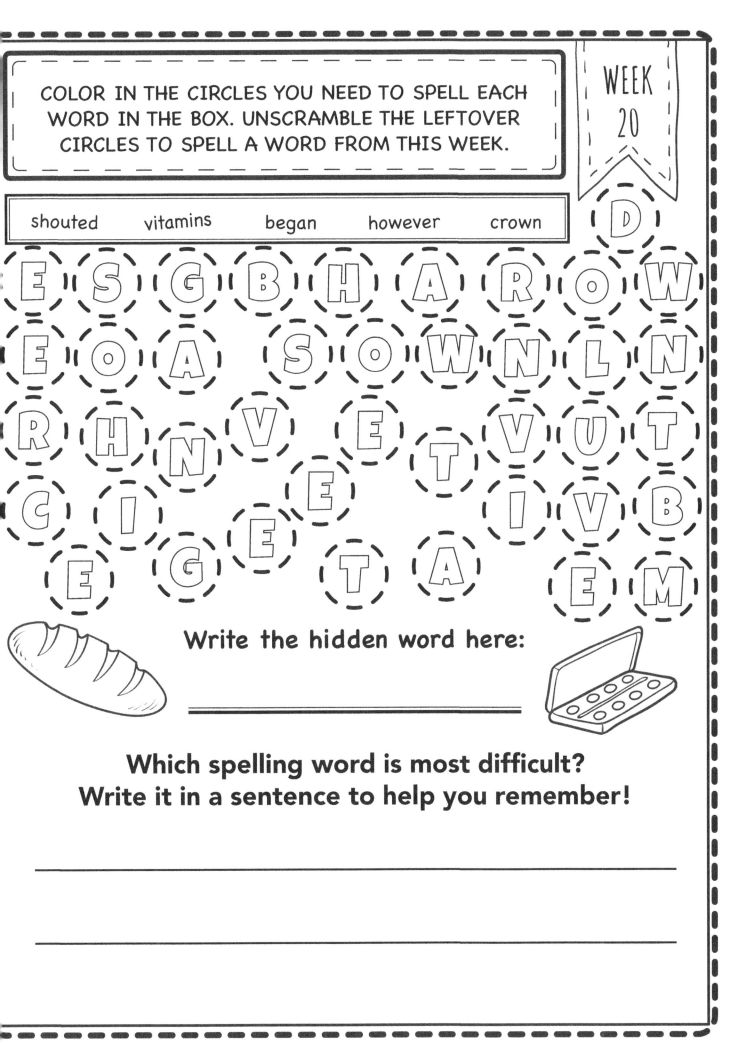

Write the hidden word here:

Which spelling word is most difficult?
Write it in a sentence to help you remember!

Color the word in each row that rhymes with the word on the left

OWL	fish	bottle	growl
SHOOK	music	took	zoo
DELIVER	river	apple	stripe
RAN	desert	began	sand
CLOWN	could	crown	enough
SOUND	circus	melody	around

WEEK 21

SPELLING WORDS

1. fountain
2. ground
3. pounds
4. account
5. drought
6. remainder
7. object
8. sleep
9. carry
10. north

Circle each spelling word in the word search.
Write each word twice in the blank spaces below as you find it.

M	X	C	C	E	J	P	B	W	A	J	H
G	I	C	A	R	R	Y	I	X	T	A	T
H	R	Q	H	H	O	X	C	G	C	C	F
M	A	O	T	R	X	M	X	Z	E	C	O
L	F	R	U	U	P	T	V	G	J	O	U
J	O	C	T	N	H	O	S	K	B	U	N
N	O	H	U	G	D	M	U	C	O	N	T
J	L	L	U	S	Q	H	H	N	F	T	A
V	K	O	L	Z	W	Y	V	H	D	V	I
F	R	E	M	A	I	N	D	E	R	S	N
D	E	I	Q	J	S	U	H	T	D	Y	Q
P	J	X	P	H	E	C	A	I	T	S	Z

1 _____ _____

2 _____ _____

3 _____ _____

4 _____ _____

5 _____ _____

6 _____ _____

7 _____ _____

8 _____ _____

9 _____ _____

10 _____ _____

1. Put each word into alphabetical order by writing it on the dashed line.
2. Get creative and write your own sentence for each word!

WEEK
21

1) ------------ _____

_____

2) ------------ _____

_____

3) ------------ _____

_____

4) ------------ _____

_____

5) ------------ _____

_____

6) ------------ _____

_____

7) ------------ _____

_____

8) ------------ _____

_____

9) ------------ _____

_____

10) ------------ _____

_____

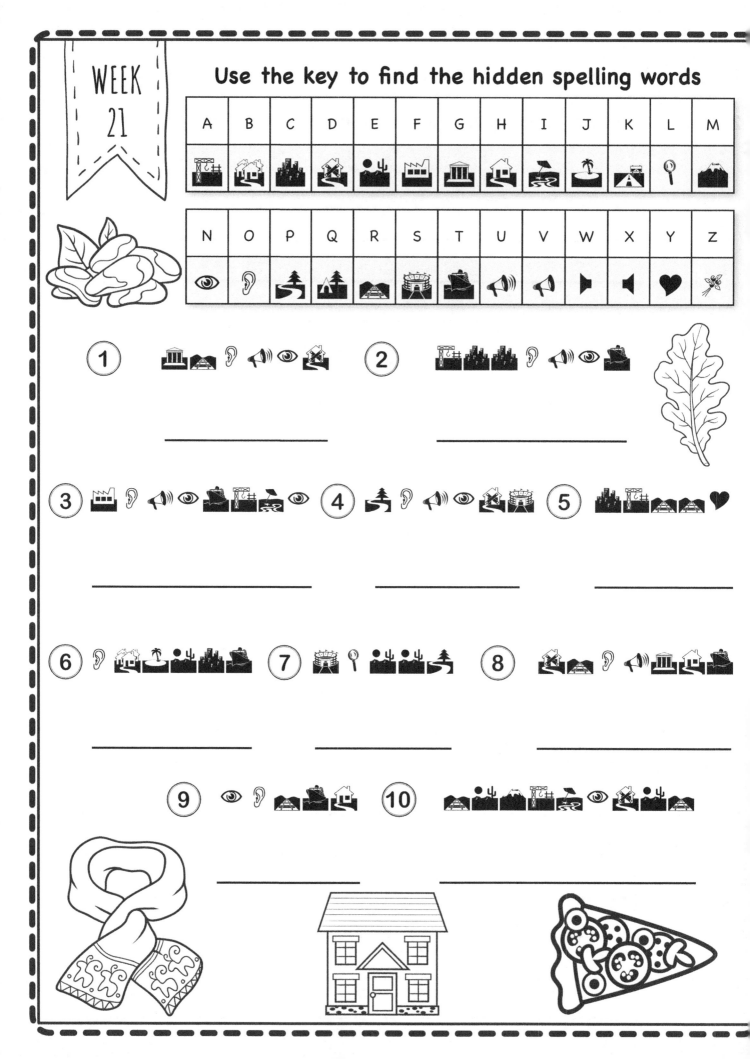

WEEK 21

Use the key to find the hidden spelling words

A	B	C	D	E	F	G	H	I	J	K	L	M

N	O	P	Q	R	S	T	U	V	W	X	Y	Z

1 _____

2 _____

3 _____

4 _____

5 _____

6 _____

7 _____

8 _____

9 _____

10 _____

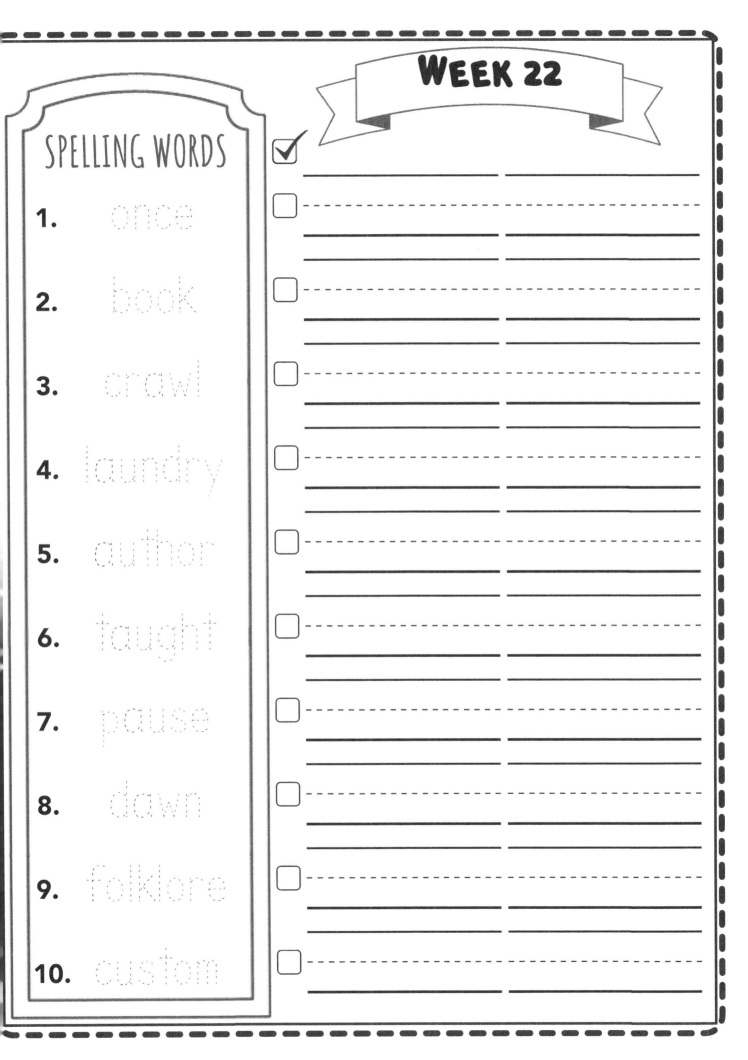

WEEK 22

SPELLING WORDS

1. once
2. book
3. crawl
4. laundry
5. author
6. taught
7. pause
8. dawn
9. folklore
10. custom

Use the clues below to fill out the crossword with the spelling words. Write the word again on the blank line.

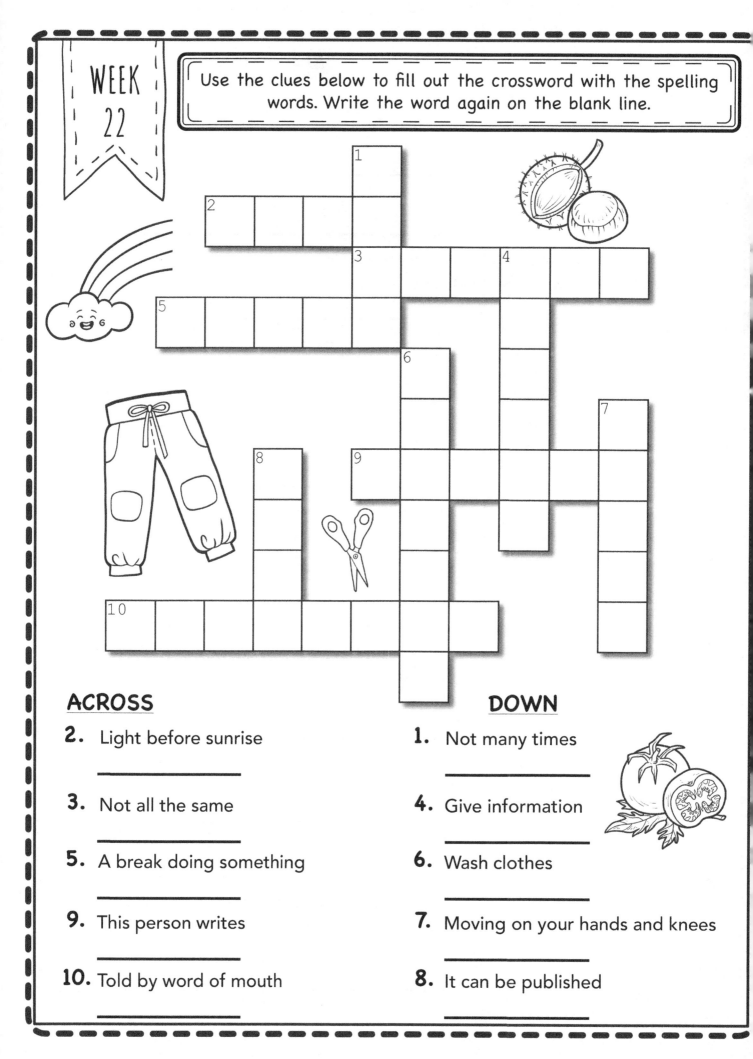

ACROSS

2. Light before sunrise

_____

3. Not all the same

_____

5. A break doing something

_____

9. This person writes

_____

10. Told by word of mouth

_____

DOWN

1. Not many times

_____

4. Give information

_____

6. Wash clothes

_____

7. Moving on your hands and knees

_____

8. It can be published

_____

Put all of the spelling words
into alphabetical order

WEEK
22

1. _____

2. _____

3. _____

4. _____

5. _____

6. _____

7. _____

8. _____

9. _____

10. _____

Start at any letter and move around the
circle to find one of the spelling words. Circle
the first letter then write the full word below

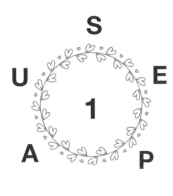

S
U   E
1
A   P

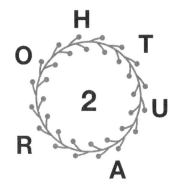

H
O   T
2
R   U
A

_____   _____

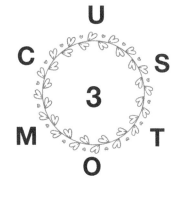

U
C   S
3
M   T
O

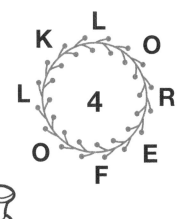

L
K   O
L   4   R
O   E
F

_____   _____

A
U   L
5
N   Y
D   R

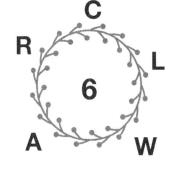

C
R   L
6
A   W

_____   _____

WEEK 22

This whale wants to soar above the clouds! Fill in each balloon with a spelling word from this week then have fun coloring!

WEEK 23

SPELLING WORDS

1. disappear
2. willow
3. traditional
4. south
5. sir
6. without
7. second
8. birds
9. loose
10. choose

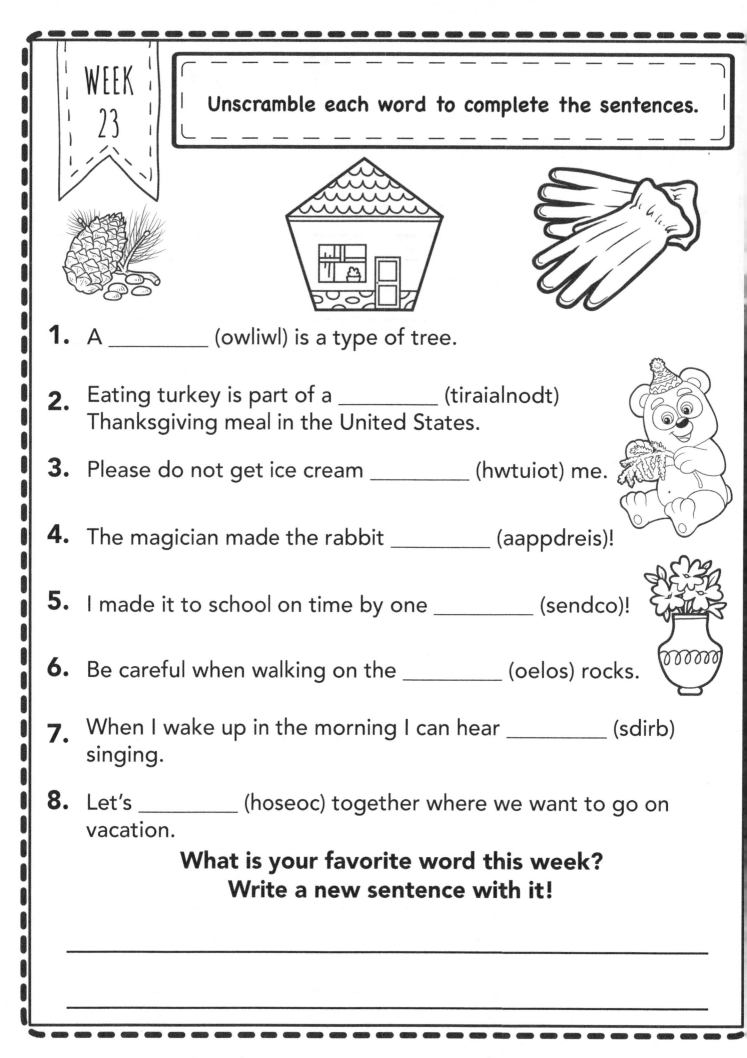

WEEK 23

Unscramble each word to complete the sentences.

1. A _____ (owliwl) is a type of tree.

2. Eating turkey is part of a _____ (tiraialnodt) Thanksgiving meal in the United States.

3. Please do not get ice cream _____ (hwtuiot) me.

4. The magician made the rabbit _____ (aappdreis)!

5. I made it to school on time by one _____ (sendco)!

6. Be careful when walking on the _____ (oelos) rocks.

7. When I wake up in the morning I can hear _____ (sdirb) singing.

8. Let's _____ (hoseoc) together where we want to go on vacation.

What is your favorite word this week?
Write a new sentence with it!

_____

_____

COLOR IN THE CIRCLES YOU NEED TO SPELL EACH
WORD IN THE BOX. UNSCRAMBLE THE LEFTOVER
CIRCLES TO SPELL A WORD FROM THIS WEEK.

WEEK
23

W

choose   second   south   without   willow   choose

O L I A W T H I T
A C H D N O O S E
O U U N L E T W O
T R E D I S O C H
O L S C T O S O H I

Write the hidden word here:

_____

Which spelling word is most difficult?
Write it in a sentence to help you remember!

_____

_____

Circle each spelling word in the word search.
Write each word twice in the blank spaces below as you find it.

R	O	M	S	B	I	R	D	S	H	R	Z
V	R	A	E	P	P	A	S	I	D	R	T
O	B	M	C	S	R	I	S	Z	L	Z	J
Q	Z	S	O	T	L	S	I	N	B	L	L
U	X	U	N	Z	L	O	O	S	E	O	G
C	T	Q	D	W	I	T	H	O	U	T	C
H	C	Z	W	Y	F	B	U	R	C	U	A
M	L	A	N	O	I	T	I	D	A	R	T
Z	K	H	U	Q	L	C	H	O	O	S	E
I	B	S	M	L	J	L	R	L	M	G	E
Z	F	L	G	K	X	Z	I	U	J	H	V
P	Z	P	P	H	L	Q	F	W	R	U	Y

1 _____ _____

2 _____ _____

3 _____ _____

4 _____ _____

5 _____

6 _____ _____

7 _____ _____

8 _____ _____

9 _____ _____

10 _____ _____

SPELLING WORDS

1. shook
2. understood
3. balloon
4. looked
5. moose
6. wheel
7. season
8. axle
9. momentum
10. miss

Correctly spell the words by filling in the blanks with the missing letters. Letters from the box below can be used more than once.

R S N W T N O L M E

__H__ __L   U__DE__ __TA__D

__OM__N__U__   SH__OK

M__OS__   BA__L__ __N

S__AS__N   L__OK__ __

Look at the letters in the shapes and then answer the questions below

a   l   s   s   s
          m e   e   i
     e d   o o   r u x
m   n   o   t s d

1. What word can you make with the letters in the triangle?

_____

2. What word can you make with the letters in the rectangle?

_____

3. What two words can you make with the letters outside both shapes?

_____ _____

1. Put each word into alphabetical order by writing it on the dashed line.
2. Get creative and write your own sentence for each word!

① - - - - - - - - - - _____

_____

② - - - - - - - - - _____

_____

③ - - - - - - - - - - _____

_____

④ - - - - - - - - _____

_____

⑤ - - - - - - - - - _____

_____

⑥ - - - - - - - - _____

_____

⑦ - - - - - - - - - _____

_____

⑧ - - - - - - - - _____

_____

⑨ - - - - - - - - _____

_____

⑩ - - - - - - - - - _____

_____

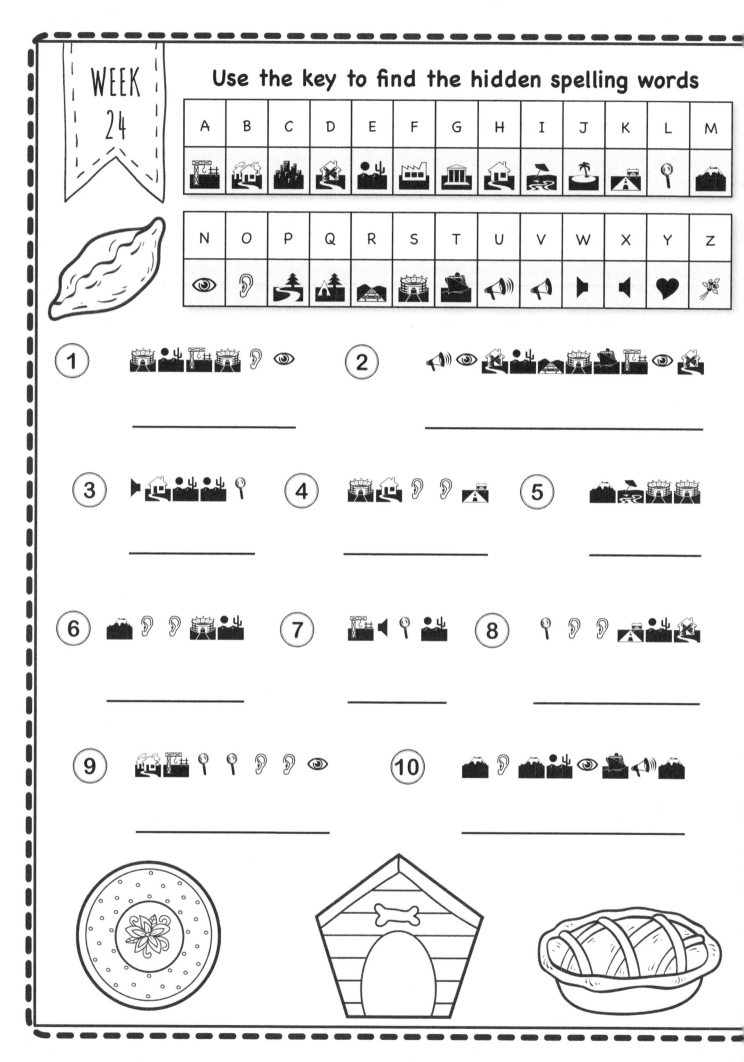

WEEK 24

Use the key to find the hidden spelling words

A	B	C	D	E	F	G	H	I	J	K	L	M

N	O	P	Q	R	S	T	U	V	W	X	Y	Z

1

2

3

4

5

6

7

8

9

10

WEEK 25

SPELLING WORDS

1. idea
2. copy
3. poor
4. floor
5. started
6. stars
7. carpet
8. marker
9. party
10. pardon

1. Fill in each blank by unscrambling the words below.
2. Use the letters shown in the crossword to help you fill in the rest of the puzzle with this week's spelling words.

OPDRAN   _____

RYAPT   _____

KERRMA   _____

PTCRAE   _____

STRSA   _____

STDRETA   _____

OFLOR   _____

ORPO   _____

PCOY   _____

ADIE   _____

COLOR IN THE CIRCLES YOU NEED TO SPELL EACH
WORD IN THE BOX. UNSCRAMBLE THE LEFTOVER
CIRCLES TO SPELL A WORD FROM THIS WEEK.

WEEK
25

pardon   started   floor   idea   carpet   party   stars

E M F I D P O N A S T
O O S R T K D E A Y
L R A S P R R R R C
T E E P A T D A A
R T

Write the hidden word here:

A R

_____

**Which spelling word is most difficult?
Write it in a sentence to help you remember!**

_____

_____

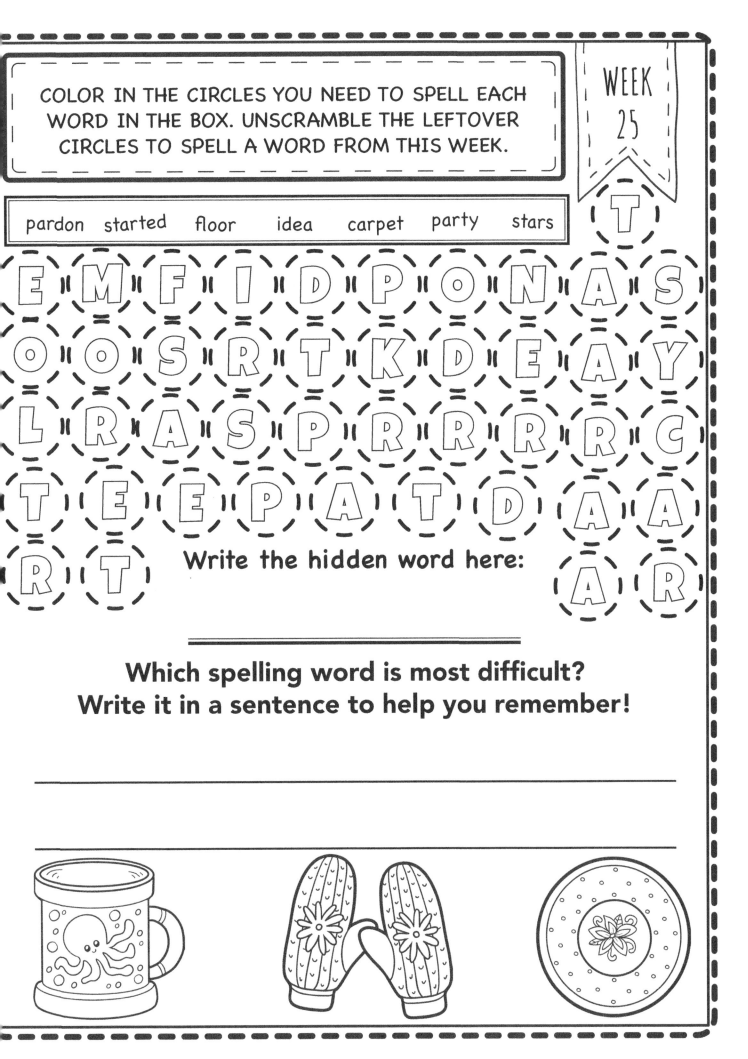

WEEK 25

Put all of the spelling words into alphabetical order

Start at any letter and move around the circle to find one of the spelling words. Circle the first letter then write the full word below

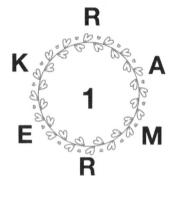

R K A E R M
1

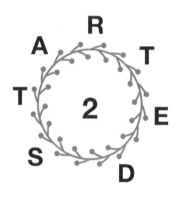

A R T T E S D
2

_____

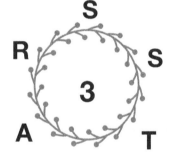

S R S A T
3

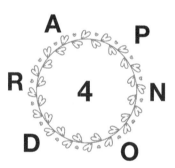

A P R N D O
4

_____

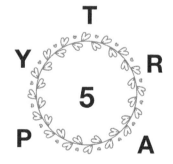

T Y R P A
5

T C E A P R
6

_____

1. _____

2. _____

3. _____

4. _____

5. _____

6. _____

7. _____

8. _____

9. _____

10. _____

EXTRA PRACTICE

1. Write your favorite spelling words from this book on the turtle shell.
2. Get creative and have fun coloring!

Get a friend or family member to choose any spelling words from this book and say them aloud. Test your memory and spelling skills by writing them down below!

Spelling Practice

1. _____
2. _____
3. _____
4. _____
5. _____
6. _____
7. _____
8. _____
9. _____
10. _____

Spelling Practice

1. _____
2. _____
3. _____
4. _____
5. _____
6. _____
7. _____
8. _____
9. _____
10. _____

Spelling Practice

1. _____
2. _____
3. _____
4. _____
5. _____
6. _____
7. _____
8. _____
9. _____
10. _____

Get a friend or family member to choose any spelling words from this book and say them aloud. Test your memory and spelling skills by writing them down below!

Spelling Practice

1. _____

2. _____

3. _____

4. _____

5. _____

6. _____

7. _____

8. _____

9. _____

10. _____

Spelling Practice

1. _____

2. _____

3. _____

4. _____

5. _____

6. _____

7. _____

8. _____

9. _____

10. _____

Spelling Practice

1. _____

2. _____

3. _____

4. _____

5. _____

6. _____

7. _____

8. _____

9. _____

10. _____

Get a friend or family member to choose any spelling words from this book and say them aloud. Test your memory and spelling skills by writing them down below!

Spelling Practice

1. _____
2. _____
3. _____
4. _____
5. _____
6. _____
7. _____
8. _____
9. _____
10. _____

Spelling Practice

1. _____
2. _____
3. _____
4. _____
5. _____
6. _____
7. _____
8. _____
9. _____
10. _____

Spelling Practice

1. _____
2. _____
3. _____
4. _____
5. _____
6. _____
7. _____
8. _____
9. _____
10. _____

ANSWER KEY

We love trees, which is why we've made the answer key digital.

Visit the below link to get it:

https://bit.ly/3VjvNwP

OR

Made in the USA
Las Vegas, NV
13 November 2024

11654888R10063